Diabetic Air Fryer Cookbook #2020

80+ Affordable, Easy and Healthy Recipes for Your Air Fryer | How to Prevent, Control and Live Well with Diabetes | 30-Day Meal Plan

Teresor Highon

© Copyright 2019 Teresor Highon- All Rights Reserved.

In no way is it legal to reproduce, duplicate, or transmit any part of this document by either electronic means or in printed format. Recording of this publication is strictly prohibited, and any storage of this material is not allowed unless with written permission from the publisher. All rights reserved.

The information provided herein is stated to be truthful and consistent, in that any liability, regarding inattention or otherwise, by any usage or abuse of any policies, processes, or directions contained within is the solitary and complete responsibility of the recipient reader. Under no circumstances will any legal liability or blame be held against the publisher for any reparation, damages, or monetary loss due to the information herein, either directly or indirectly.

Respective authors own all copyrights not held by the publisher.

Legal Notice:

This book is copyright protected. This is only for personal use. You cannot amend, distribute, sell, use, quote or paraphrase any part of the content within this book without the consent of the author or copyright owner. Legal action will be pursued if this is breached.

Disclaimer Notice:

Please note the information contained within this document is for educational and entertainment purposes only. Every attempt has been made to provide accurate, up-to-date and reliable, complete information. No warranties of any kind are expressed or implied. Readers acknowledge that the author is not engaging in the rendering of legal, financial, medical or professional advice.

By reading this document, the reader agrees that under no circumstances are we responsible for any losses, direct or indirect, which are incurred as a result of the use of information contained within this document, including, but not limited to, errors, omissions, or inaccuracies.

Table of contents

Introduction 6
Chapter1: Understanding the Diabetes 7
    The link between obesity and type 2 Diabetes 7
    Types of diabetes, symptoms, and treatment 7
    A healthy meal can help ease the effects of Diabetes 9
Chapter2: Understanding the Air Fryer 12
    Advantages of using an Air Fryer 12
    How to start cooking in an Air Fryer 13
Chapter3: The Benefit of the Diabetic Air Fryer 15
Chapter4: 30-Day Meal Plan 16
Chapter5: Breakfast 19
    Tofu Scramble 19
    Fried Egg 20
    Scotch Eggs 21
    Spinach and Tomato Frittata 23
    Herb Frittata 24
    Pancakes 25
    Zucchini Bread 26
    Blueberry Muffins 28
    Baked Eggs 30
    Bagels 31
    Cauliflower Hash Browns 33
    Cornbread 34
Chapter 6: Poultry 35
    Caribbean Spiced Chicken 35
    Chicken Sandwich 37
    Buttermilk Fried Chicken 39
    Chicken Wings 41
    Chicken Tenders 42

Chicken Nuggets	43
Chicken Meatballs	45
Buffalo Chicken Hot Wings	46
Herb Chicken Thighs	47
Lemon Pepper Chicken	49

Chapter 7: Appetizers and Siders 50

Ravioli	50
Onion Rings	52
Cauliflower Fritters	54
Zucchini Fritters	55
Kale Chips	56
Radish Chips	57
Zucchini Fries	58
Avocado fries	59
Roasted Peanut Butter Squash	60
Roasted Chickpeas	61

Chapter 8: Beef, Pork and Lamb 62

Pork Chops	62
Steak	64
Meatloaf Slider Wraps	65
Pork Belly	66
Sirloin Steak	67
Vietnamese Grilled Pork	68
Meatloaf	70
Herbed Lamb Chops	71
Spicy Lamb Sirloin Steak	73
Garlic Rosemary Lamb Chops	75
Double Cheeseburger	76
Steak Bites with Mushrooms	77

Chapter 9: Vegetarian 78

Cabbage Wedges	78

- Buffalo Cauliflower Wings ... 80
- Sweet Potato Cauliflower Patties ... 81
- Okra ... 83
- Creamed Spinach ... 84
- Eggplant Parmesan ... 85
- Cauliflower Rice ... 87
- Brussels Sprouts ... 89
- Green Beans ... 90
- Asparagus Avocado Soup ... 91

Chapter 10: Fish and Seafood ... 92
- Crab Cake ... 92
- Salmon ... 93
- Parmesan Shrimp ... 94
- Fish Sticks ... 95
- Shrimp with Lemon and Chile ... 96
- Tilapia ... 97
- Tomato Basil Scallops ... 98
- Shrimp Scampi ... 99
- Salmon Cakes ... 100
- Cilantro Lime Shrimps ... 101

Chapter 11: Dessert ... 102
- Cheesecake Bites ... 102
- Coconut Pie ... 103
- Crustless Cheesecake ... 104
- Chocolate Cake ... 105
- Chocolate Brownies ... 106
- Spiced Apples ... 107
- Sweet Potato Fries ... 108
- Chocolate Lava Cake ... 109

Conclusion ... 110

Introduction

Diabetes is a common yet serious health condition. It is characterized by an elevated level of blood glucose in blood, which results from defect in insulin production and/or insulin action. People who have obese or those who eat fatty food are at higher risk of developing diabetes.

If you have diabetes, overweight, or health-conscious, eating fatty foods or high-calorie foods would cause diabetes.

Does this mean you can no longer eat fried fatty food?

Yes, you can, all thanks to the air fryer.

The air fryer is the modern kitchen tool that is proving its worth in effectively reducing the risk of diabetes, weight loss and living a healthier life, without compromising on the fried, fatty and high-calorie food.

Read on to know how air fryer has turned out to be a blessing for a person with diabetes.

Chapter 1: Understanding the Diabetes

According to the CDC, there are more than 30 million individuals in America that have diabetes; and 1 in 4 of these people don't know they have this condition. The cause of diabetes is linked with the pancreases, which fail to produce or use insulin properly. Insulin hormone is secreted into the bloodstream by the pancreatic gland to deliver it into the cells. Once, the cells take in the sugar, it is then converted into energy and use immediately or store for later use.

The link between obesity and type 2 Diabetes

Although the exact cause of type 2 diabetes is still not fully understood, being obese and overweight is believed to account 80 percent of the risk of developing diabetes. So, if you have excess weight around your tummy, you are at greater risk of developing type 2 diabetes. In obese people, the abdominal fat cells have to more nutrients than average, and then this stress in the cell makes them release pro-inflammatory chemicals. These chemicals disrupt the function of insulin hormone and/or makes the body less sensitive to the insulin. This is known as insulin resistance which is the major cause of type 2 diabetes. Therefore, having excess abdominal fat or large waistline leads to high risk of diabetes.

Types of diabetes, symptoms, and treatment

There are two main types of diabetes – type 1 diabetes and type 2 diabetes. How can you tell if you have diabetes and which one? The differences between them are their causes.

Type 1 diabetes:

It's autoimmune diseases that cause insulin to destroy the beta cells of pancreases. It is caused by a fault in the immune response of the body, triggered by a virus, which mistakenly led the body to target and destroy beta cells of the pancreases, which are responsible for producing insulin. Hence, the loss of these cells prevents the body to produce enough insulin to control the blood sugar levels, and the symptoms of diabetes begin to appear.

Signs of type 1 diabetes: This type of diabetes tends to develop more in over 35 years old adults than in children. The warning signs of type 1 diabetes include increased thirst, dry mouth, peeing more often, itchy skin, weight loss, tiredness during the day, and genital itchiness. If your body shows any of these signs, then there are chances that you have developed diabetes. Consult a doctor immediately and he may do urine and blood test to confirm if you have actually developed diabetes.

Treatment of type 1 diabetes: As the killing of beta cells reduce insulin in the body, it is the treatment for this condition – insulin treatment. Individuals suffering from type 1 diabetes treat this condition by injecting insulin in the body with insulin pen and insulin pump. These insulin doses are also balanced with dietary intake, physical activities and regular monitoring of blood glucose level that will help you control your diabetes. As mentioned before, exercise and eating healthy meals are important for minimizing the harmful effects of diabetes like retinopathy, kidney diseases, heart diseases, and stroke, etc. However, delivering insulin in the body, proper dietary intake along with exercise only helps to maintain good blood glucose level, not elevating or reversing type 1 diabetes.

Type 2 diabetes:

High blood glucose level results in type 2 diabetes. Under this condition, the body becomes insulin resistant which is body becoming ineffective to use insulin hormone and/or it becomes unable to produce insulin. Insulin hormone is needed for cell to take in glucose (simple sugar) from the blood and then convert it into energy. In type 2 diabetes, body is unable to metabolize the simple sugar or glucose, which leads to high blood glucose level over time that may damage organs of the body. From this, food for individuals suffering from this type of diabetes becomes a sort of poison. But these people can stay well by lowering their blood sugar by avoiding foods that are high in sugar and using some medications.

Signs of Type 2 diabetes: The signs of type 2 diabetes are increased urination, increased thirst, and hunger, unintended loss of muscle mass, extreme tiredness, blurred vision, slow healing of sores, frequent infections, and darkened skin under mock and armpits. These symptoms are similar to type 1 diabetes; however, these signs develop more slowly in type 2 diabetes-like over the months and years and hence, it becomes harder to identify these signs of diabetes.

Risks of Type 2 diabetes: There are a number of factors that increases the risk of developing type 2 diabetes including overweight, consuming unhealthy foods, less physical activity, raised blood pressure, high cholesterol level, smoking, etc. Moreover, environmental factors, family history, age of over 45 years, and belonging to certain races like Asian-American, black, American Indian and Hispanic also influenced the likelihood of developing diabetes.

Treatment of Type 2 diabetes: Irrespective to type 1 diabetes, type 2 diabetes can be prevented if detected and treated at an early stage. The common treatment for type 2 diabetes includes consuming low carb, high fiber and low glycemic index diet along with appropriate and regular physical activities. Some medicines may also be prescribed to diabetic patients like metformin that is the most common drug for type 2 diabetes patients and helps the body to respond better to insulin.

A healthy meal can help ease the effects of Diabetes

What you eat matter most when you have diabetes. Good news is that nothing is off-limits and even the items which you consider as 'bad' for you could be taken in tiny amounts as occasional treats. Still, it's better to stick to best food options to easily manage your diabetes.

- Starches

What to eat – The best options are to eat whole grains like millet, oatmeal, quinoa, barley, brown rice, amaranth and high fiber cereals, flours such as coconut flour, almond flour, hazelnut flours, and no or very little added sugar.
What to avoid – Avoid processed grains like white flour, baked goods made with white flour like white bread, white rice, white pasta, crackers, pretzels, cereals with lots of sugar, white breads, white flour tortilla, etc.

- Vegetables

What to eat – You need to eat vegetables that have fewer carbs and lots of fibers, and this includes all fresh and/or frozen vegetables, especially leafy greens. You can eat them raw and have them as roasted, grilled or steamed. You can also use canned vegetables in your meal but make sure they are unsalted or have low sodium.
What to avoid – Worst choices of vegetables include canned veggies with high sodium, vegetables cooked with lots of high-fat cheeses, butter or sauce, and high sodium pickles.

- Fruits

What to eat – Eat fruits that are low in fat and sodium and high in fiber, minerals and vitamins like berries, pears, apples, oranges, etc. But fruits tend to have more carbohydrates than vegetables. The best choices for fruits are fresh fruits, frozen fruits, or canned fruits without any sugar. Similarly, you can eat low-sugar or sugar-free jam and apple sauce.

What to avoid – Avoid eating fruits that have a high glycemic index, canned fruits that are packed in heavy sugar syrup, sweetened applesauce, and regular jelly, jam, and preserves. Avoid taking sweetened fruit punches, drinks, juices, and alcoholic drinks.

- Proteins

What to eat – Include plant-based proteins in your meals like chickpeas, beans, nuts, and seeds. You can also consume grass-fed beef, pastured chicken, pork and lamb, wild-caught fish in moderate amount. You can get protein from vegan meat options like tofu and seitan. Add pastured eggs and low-fat cheeses in your food to meet your protein requirements.

What to avoid – Avoid fried and higher fat meat cuts, regular cheeses, poultry with skin, deep-fried tofu and fish and beans prepared using lard.

- Dairy

What to eat – Use low-fat dairy but in small portions and this include skim or reduced-fat milk, low-fat yogurt, low-fat cheeses, and non-fat sour cream.

What to avoid – Don't use whole milk, regular milk, sweetened yogurt, cheeses, sour cream, half-and-half, and ice creams.

- Fats, Oils, and Sweets

What to eat – Use natural sources of fats like from vegetables like eating nuts, seeds, olives, avocado, reduced-fat dips and dressing, and plant-based oils like olive oil, canola oil, grapeseed oil, and low-fat butter. You can also eat high-fat fishes like tuna, salmon, and mackerel as these foods are rich in omega-3 fatty acids. For sweetness, use dried fruits or sugar substitute like coconut sugar, erythritol, swerve, stevia, etc.

What to avoid – Avoid every food that has trans-fat as it is bad for heart health, even if the nutritional label says the food contains 0 gram of trans fat. Also, avoid big portions of saturated fats like coconut oil, palm oil or from animal products. Don't eat fries, potato chips, most fast foods, and premade meals.

- Drinks

What to eat – The best options for drinks include lots of water, unflavored water, unsweetened tea and black coffee, coffee with low-fat milk, flavored sparkling water, non-fruity drinks, fresh and unsweetened fruit juices, and a small amount of wines. Read the labels of the drink to know what is being served to you.

What to avoid – Avoid drinking regular sodas, fruity mixed drinks, wines, sweetened tea, sweetened coffee with high-fat milk and cream, flavored drinks, chocolate drinks, sodas, energy drinks and sweetener such a table sugar, maple syrup, agave nectar, etc.

Chapter 2: Understanding the Air Fryer

The air fryer has become the most popular and trendy kitchen appliance this year. But why are people excited about it? Why has it become favorite of people who love fried food? Why is it promoting frying being healthy?

The air fryer is nothing like a typical deep fryer. This cooking utensil is much more like a small, stylish and self-contained oven that uses convection cooking method. It uses electrical element that heats the air in the fryer and then circulates it evenly around the food for its cooking. As a result, this hot air cooks the food in the fryer quickly and brings out the well-cooked food that is evenly browned and crunchy on the outside, but the inside of food stays moist and tasty.

Advantages of using an Air Fryer

- Healthier Cooking

With air fryer, frying your food is healthy. How? Air fryer only needs just a tiny sprit of oil or no oil at all to cook your cook. You can easily cook fries, chicken wings, onion rings and much more and still get crispy foods without the extra oil. And, compare to oven and deep-frying cooking, the foods from the air fryer especially fries are crispier and not dried out, making the food even more impressive.

- Quicker Meals

Since air fryer is small than the oven, it circulates hot air around its fan quickly that cooks the food faster. Air fryer takes less time to reach the cooking temperature compare to an oven which may take 20 minutes or more to properly preheat and begin cooking. So, if you need to make your meals in a hurry, you will love the air fryer time-saving features.

- Versatility

Air fryer doesn't only just do frying. You can do so much more cooking with it! The air fryer can also roast, grill, stir-fry, broil and bakes, even cakes. You can make fresh or frozen food in it, or reheat the leftovers. Make use of air fryer additional accessories like cake pan, pizza pan, rotisserie rack, frill pan, steamer inserts to cook variety of foods.

- Space Saver

If you live in a dorm, share house, or have a small kitchen, then you will definitely appreciate the small size of air fryer. The air fryer comes in different sizes, but its small size can be of a coffee maker size, which won't take too much room on your kitchen counter. Hence, air fryer is easy to move or store away. The air fryer is also handy to take it on your travel ventures and placing it in your office kitchen to cook fresh food.

- Ease of Clean up

Most of the cooks don't enjoy the cleanup of kitchen utensils, but with air fryer, this won't be a trouble for you in any way. Air fryer just has a fryer basket and pan to clean, which is dishwasher safe and takes few minutes to wash up after cooking. And, the cooking basket or pan is non-stick, so food usually doesn't stick to it and instead, slides onto the plate easily.

How to start cooking in an Air Fryer

Here's how you can start cooking with your air fryer and get most of it.

- Adjust the cooking temperature

Although there are many air frying recipes and at the beginning of your air fryer cooking, you should stick to them to understand how air fryer cooking works and proficient air frying cooking skills. Then, move on to convert your regular deep frying or oven-baked recipes into air frying one. For this, reduce the cooking temperature by 25 degrees F to achieve the same result in terms of texture and taste of your food. For example, if your recipe is deep-fried in the oil heated to 350 degrees F, then air fryer the same food at 325 degrees F. This rule applies to other converting recipes, be it baking, roasting, broiling, etc. Remember to pre-heat your air fryer to temperature 220 degrees F or recipe suggested temperature, it usually takes 5 minutes, and then fill the frying basket for further cooking.

- Toss the ingredients with oil

Although the cooking accessories of the air fryer are non-stick, still you should toss your food ingredients in oil, about 1 to 2 tablespoons. You can skip this step for foods that are naturally fatty like meatballs. And, for foods that are coated in flour or battered, cook them in greased frying basket and then coat the top of food with an oil spray. This oil is essential to make sure that air fried food turns out golden-brown, crunchy and appealing.

- Filling the frying basket

Foods coated with flour or battered should be fry in one layer in the air fryer. For foods like fries or vegetables, you can load the frying basket to the top, but a full basket takes a long cooking time and may result in food that is not quite crispy. It is also recommended to shake the basket at least twice to make sure food is cook evenly.

- Check the doneness early

Circulation of hot air in the air fryer helps in maintaining a consistent temperature in the air fryer, which tends to cook the food faster than being cooked in conventional oven and deep fryer. This means that if you are converting your regular food into an air fryer one or the recipe you have already cooked in an air fryer, you will need to check the food about two-third of the suggested cooking time to test its doneness. For example, if fish sticks recipe says to be cook in 15 minutes, then start checking them at 10 minutes.

Chapter 3: The Benefit of the Diabetic Air Fryer

Many studies have pinpointed that fried foods are bad for health and wellbeing. But, the cooking method in air fryer promotes healthier way to fry food, without compromising its taste and crunchiness. And, this makes air fryer good for health-conscious individuals and diabetics.

Here's why?

The main reason for this claim is the use of less oil in cooking foods with an air fryer, and this cut up to 80 percent of the fat compared to deep fryer. Isn't that huge?! And, the fried foods in it has similar taste and texture to regular deep-fried foods.

Furthermore, studies have confirmed that consuming too much fried foods increases the risks of obesity in adults. The more you consume fried food, the more you will have the risk of developing diabetes. However, if you consume fried foods often, it can risk your health with type 2 diabetes. Thus, to lower the intake of fats and/or to lose weight without cutting down your fried food diet, you should switch to air fried cooking. Air fryer reduces the fat content, which would drastically reduce the number of calories by significant amount. For example, deep-fried chicken wings are extremely fatty, but the air fried chicken wings contain less fat and more protein.

The fewer fats and calories with preserved nutrition and ingredients are good for health freaks, weight watchers, and diabetics. Foods that are cooked in the deep fryer have more calorie and fats compared to the ones that are prepared in the air fryer. And, these fats and calories are way too high to be part of healthy diet. Thus, eating low-fat food prepared in air fryer impacts your health positively. As a result, it will reduce the risks of health conditions like

- Obesity
- Heart diseases
- Heart attacked
- Blocked arteries
- Internal inflammation

With this information in mind, you can understand how the air fryer benefits anyone who is trying to control or prevent diabetes and eat healthier.

Chapter 4: 30-Day Meal Plan

Day 1

Breakfast: Tofu Scramble

Lunch: Chicken Sandwich

Dinner: Cauliflower Rice

Dessert: Spiced Apples

Day 2

Breakfast: Zucchini Bread

Lunch: Steak

Dinner: Cauliflower Rice

Dessert: Spiced Apples

Day 3

Breakfast: Zucchini Bread

Lunch: Crab Cake

Dinner: Pork Chops

Dessert: Cheesecake Bites

Day 4

Breakfast: Cauliflower Hash Browns

Lunch: Crab Cake

Dinner: Buffalo Cauliflower Wings

Dessert: Cheesecake Bites

Day 5

Breakfast: Cauliflower Hash Browns

Lunch: Chicken Nuggets

Dinner: Buffalo Cauliflower Wings

Dessert: Cheesecake Bites

Day 6

Breakfast: Fried Egg

Lunch: Cabbage Wedges

Dinner: Parmesan Shrimp

Dessert: Cheesecake Bites

Day 7

Breakfast: Bagels

Lunch: Zucchini Fritters

Dinner: Chicken Meatballs

Dessert: Chocolate Cake

Day 8

Breakfast: Bagels

Lunch: Meatloaf Slider Wraps

Dinner: Chicken Meatballs

Dessert: Chocolate Cake

Day 9

Breakfast: Spinach and Tomato Frittata

Lunch: Meatloaf Slider Wraps

Dinner: Spicy Lamb Sirloin Steak

Dessert: Chocolate Cake

Day 10

Breakfast: Spinach and Tomato Frittata

Lunch: Shrimp with Lemon and Chile

Dinner: Creamed Spinach

Dessert: Chocolate Cake

Day 11

Breakfast: Spinach and Tomato Frittata

Lunch: Buffalo Chicken Hot Wings

Dinner: Tomato Basil Scallops

Dessert: Sweet Potato Fries

Day 12

Breakfast: Spinach and Tomato Frittata

Lunch: Sweet Potato Cauliflower Patties

Dinner: Chicken Wings

Dessert: Sweet Potato Fries

Day 13

Breakfast: Pancakes

Lunch: Sweet Potato Cauliflower Patties

Dinner: Cilantro Lime Shrimps

Dessert: Coconut Pie

Day 14

Breakfast: Pancakes

Lunch: Herbed Lamb Chops

Dinner: Eggplant Parmesan

Dessert: Coconut Pie

Day 15

Breakfast: Blueberry Muffins

Lunch: Salmon Cakes

Dinner: Shrimp Scampi

Dessert: Coconut Pie

Day 16

Breakfast: Blueberry Muffins

Lunch: Salmon Cakes

Dinner: Roasted Peanut Butter Squash

Dessert: Coconut Pie

Day 17

Breakfast: Scotch Eggs

Lunch: Roasted Chickpeas

Dinner: Steak Bites with Mushrooms

Dessert: Chocolate Brownies

Day 18

Breakfast: Herb Frittata

Lunch: Buttermilk Fried Chicken

Dinner: Steak Bites with Mushrooms

Dessert: Chocolate Brownies

Day 19

Breakfast: Herb Frittata

Lunch: Meatloaf

Dinner: Chicken Tenders

Dessert: Chocolate Brownies

Day 20

Breakfast: Herb Frittata

Lunch: Meatloaf

Dinner: Chicken Tenders

Dessert: Chocolate Brownies

Day 21
Breakfast: Herb Frittata
Lunch: Cauliflower Fritters
Dinner: Eggplant Parmesan
Dessert: Crustless Cheesecake

Day 22
Breakfast: Cornbread
Lunch: Pork Belly
Dinner: Eggplant Parmesan
Dessert: Crustless Cheesecake

Day 23
Breakfast: Cornbread
Lunch: Pork Belly
Dinner: Herb Chicken Thighs
Dessert: Crustless Cheesecake

Day 24
Breakfast: Baked Eggs
Lunch: Lemon Pepper Chicken
Dinner: Garlic Rosemary Lamb Chops
Dessert: Crustless Cheesecake

Day 25
Breakfast: Tofu Scramble
Lunch: Double Cheeseburger
Dinner: Garlic Rosemary Lamb Chops
Dessert: Chocolate Lava Cake

Day 26
Breakfast: Cauliflower Hash Browns
Lunch: Tilapia
Dinner: Herb Chicken Thighs
Dessert: Chocolate Lava Cake

Day 27
Breakfast: Cauliflower Hash Browns
Lunch: Brussels Sprouts
Dinner: Asparagus Avocado Soup
Dessert: Chocolate Lava Cake

Day 28
Breakfast: Bagels
Lunch: Caribbean Spiced Chicken
Dinner: Asparagus Avocado Soup
Dessert: Chocolate Lava Cake

Day 29
Breakfast: Pancakes
Lunch: Caribbean Spiced Chicken
Dinner: Salmon
Dessert: Spiced Apples

Day 30
Breakfast: Fried Egg
Lunch: Vietnamese Grilled Pork
Dinner: Green Beans
Dessert: Cheesecake Bites

Chapter 5: Breakfast

Tofu Scramble

Preparation time: 5 minutes
Cooking time: 18 minutes
Servings: 3

Ingredients:

- 12 ounces tofu, extra-firm, drained, ½-inch cubed
- 1 teaspoon garlic powder
- 1 teaspoon onion powder
- 1 teaspoon paprika
- 1/2 teaspoon ground black pepper
- 1/2 teaspoon salt
- 1 tablespoon olive oil
- 2 teaspoon xanthan gum

Method:

1. Switch on the air fryer, insert fryer basket, grease it with olive oil, then shut with its lid, set the fryer at 220 degrees F and preheat for 5 minutes.
2. Meanwhile, place tofu pieces in a bowl, drizzle with oil, and sprinkle with xanthan gum and toss until well coated.
3. Add remaining ingredients to the tofu and then toss until well coated.
4. Open the fryer, add tofu in it, close with its lid and cook for 13 minutes until nicely golden and crispy, shaking the basket every 5 minutes.
5. When air fryer beeps, open its lid, transfer tofu onto a serving plate and serve.

Nutrition Value:

- Calories: 94 Cal
- Carbs: 5 g
- Fat: 5 g
- Protein: 6 g
- Fiber: 0 g

Fried Egg

Preparation time: 5 minutes
Cooking time: 4 minutes
Servings: 1

Ingredients:

- 1 egg, pastured
- 1/8 teaspoon salt
- 1/8 teaspoon cracked black pepper

Method:

1. Take the fryer pan, grease it with olive oil and then crack the egg in it.
2. Switch on the air fryer, insert fryer pan, then shut with its lid, and set the fryer at 370 degrees F.
3. Set the frying time to 3 minutes, then when the air fryer beep, open its lid and check the egg; if egg needs more cooking, then air fryer it for another minute.
4. Transfer the egg to a serving plate, season with salt and black pepper and serve.

Nutrition Value:

- Calories: 90 Cal
- Carbs: 0.6 g
- Fat: 7 g
- Protein: 6.3 g
- Fiber: 0 g

Scotch Eggs

Preparation time: 10 minutes
Cooking time: 15 minutes
Servings: 4

Ingredients:

- 1-pound pork sausage, pastured
- 2 tablespoons chopped parsley
- 1/8 teaspoon salt
- 1/8 teaspoon grated nutmeg
- 1 tablespoon chopped chives
- 1/8 teaspoon ground black pepper
- 2 teaspoons ground mustard, and more as needed
- 4 eggs, hard-boiled, shell peeled
- 1 cup shredded parmesan cheese, low-fat

Method:

1. Switch on the air fryer, insert fryer basket, grease it with olive oil, then shut with its lid, set the fryer at 400 degrees F and preheat for 10 minutes.
2. Meanwhile, place sausage in a bowl, add salt, black pepper, parsley, chives, nutmeg, and mustard, then stir until well mixed and shape the mixture into four patties.
3. Peel each boiled egg, then place an egg on a patty and shape the meat around it until the egg has evenly covered.
4. Place cheese in a shallow dish, and then roll the egg in the cheese until covered completely with cheese; prepare remaining eggs in the same manner.
5. Then open the fryer, add eggs in it, close with its lid and cook for 15 minutes at the 400 degrees F until nicely golden and crispy, turning the eggs and spraying with oil halfway through the frying.
6. When air fryer beeps, open its lid, transfer eggs onto a serving plate and serve with mustard.

Nutrition Value:

- Calories: 533 Cal

- Carbs: 2 g
- Fat: 43 g
- Protein: 33 g
- Fiber: 1 g

Spinach and Tomato Frittata

Preparation time: 5 minutes
Cooking time: 21 minutes
Servings: 4

Ingredients:

- 4 tablespoons chopped spinach
- 4 mushrooms, sliced
- 3 cherry tomatoes, halved
- 1 green onion, sliced
- 1 tablespoon chopped parsley
- ¾ teaspoon salt
- 1 tablespoon chopped rosemary
- 4 eggs, pastured
- 3 tablespoons heavy cream, reduced-fat
- 4 tablespoons grated cheddar cheese, reduced-fat

Method:

1. Switch on the air fryer, insert fryer pan, grease it with olive oil, then shut with its lid, set the fryer at 350 degrees F and preheat for 5 minutes.
2. Meanwhile, crack eggs in a bowl, whisk in the cream until smooth, then add remaining ingredients and stir until well combined.
3. Then open the fryer, pour the frittata mixture in it, close with its lid and cook for 12 to 16 minutes until its top is nicely golden, frittata has set, and inserted toothpick into the frittata slides out clean.
4. When air fryer beeps, open its lid, transfer frittata onto a serving plate, then cut into pieces and serve.

Nutrition Value:

- Calories: 147 Cal
- Carbs: 3 g
- Fat: 11 g
- Protein: 9 g
- Fiber: 1 g

Herb Frittata

Preparation time: 10 minutes
Cooking time: 25 minutes
Servings: 4

Ingredients:

- 2 tablespoons chopped green scallions
- 1/2 teaspoon ground black pepper
- 2 tablespoons chopped cilantro
- 1/2 teaspoon salt
- 2 tablespoons chopped parsley
- 1/2 cup half and half, reduced-fat
- 4 eggs, pastured
- 1/3 cup shredded cheddar cheese, reduced-fat

Method:

1. Switch on the air fryer, insert fryer basket, grease it with olive oil, then shut with its lid, set the fryer at 330 degrees F and preheat for 10 minutes.
2. Meanwhile, take a round heatproof pan that fits into the fryer basket, grease it well with oil and set aside until required.
3. Crack the eggs in a bowl, beat in half-and-half, then add remaining ingredients, beat until well mixed and pour the mixture into prepared pan.
4. Open the fryer, place the pan in it, close with its lid and cook for 15 minutes at the 330 degrees F until its top is nicely golden, frittata has set and inserted toothpick into the frittata slides out clean.
5. When air fryer beeps, open its lid, take out the pan, then transfer frittata onto a serving plate, cut it into pieces and serve.

Nutrition Value:

- Calories: 141 Cal
- Carbs: 2 g
- Fat: 10 g
- Protein: 8 g
- Fiber: 0 g

Pancakes

Preparation time: 5 minutes
Cooking time: 29 minutes
Servings: 4

Ingredients:

- 1 1/2 cup coconut flour
- 1 teaspoon salt
- 3 1/2 teaspoons baking powder
- 1 tablespoon erythritol sweetener
- 1 1/2 teaspoon baking soda
- 3 tablespoons melted butter
- 1 1/4 cups milk, unsweetened, reduced-fat
- 1 egg, pastured

Method:

1. Switch on the air fryer, insert fryer pan, grease it with olive oil, then shut with its lid, set the fryer at 220 degrees F and preheat for 5 minutes.
2. Meanwhile, take a medium bowl, add all the ingredients in it, whisk until well blended and then let the mixture rest for 5 minutes.
3. Open the fryer, pour in some of the pancake mixture as thin as possible, close with its lid and cook for 6 minutes until nicely golden, turning the pancake halfway through the frying.
4. When air fryer beeps, open its lid, transfer pancake onto a serving plate and use the remaining batter for cooking more pancakes in the same manner.
5. Serve straight away with fresh fruits slices.

Nutrition Value:

- Calories: 237.7 Cal
- Carbs: 39.2 g
- Fat: 10.2 g
- Protein: 6.3 g
- Fiber: 1.3 g

Zucchini Bread

Preparation time: 25 minutes
Cooking time: 40 minutes
Servings: 8

Ingredients:

- ¾ cup shredded zucchini
- 1/2 cup almond flour
- 1/4 teaspoon salt
- 1/4 cup cocoa powder, unsweetened
- 1/2 cup chocolate chips, unsweetened, divided
- 6 tablespoons erythritol sweetener
- 1/2 teaspoon baking soda
- 2 tablespoons olive oil
- 1/2 teaspoon vanilla extract, unsweetened
- 2 tablespoons butter, unsalted, melted
- 1 egg, pastured

Method:

1. Switch on the air fryer, insert fryer basket, grease it with olive oil, then shut with its lid, set the fryer at 310 degrees F and preheat for 10 minutes.
2. Meanwhile, place flour in a bowl, add salt, cocoa powder, and baking soda and stir until mixed.
3. Crack the eggs in another bowl, whisk in sweetener, egg, oil, butter, and vanilla until smooth and then slowly whisk in flour mixture until incorporated.
4. Add zucchini along with 1/3 cup chocolate chips and then fold until just mixed.
5. Take a mini loaf pan that fits into the air fryer, grease it with olive oil, then pour in the prepared batter and sprinkle remaining chocolate chips on top.
6. Open the fryer, place the loaf pan in it, close with its lid and cook for 30 minutes at the 310 degrees F until inserted toothpick into the bread slides out clean.
7. When air fryer beeps, open its lid, remove the loaf pan, then place it on a wire rack and let the bread cool in it for 20 minutes.
8. Take out the bread, let it cool completely, then cut it into slices and serve.

Nutrition Value:

- Calories: 356 Cal
- Carbs: 49 g
- Fat: 17 g
- Protein: 5.1 g
- Fiber: 2.5 g

Blueberry Muffins

Preparation time: 10 minutes
Cooking time: 30 minutes
Servings: 14

Ingredients:

- 1 cup almond flour
- 1 cup frozen blueberries
- 2 teaspoons baking powder
- 1/3 cup erythritol sweetener
- 1 teaspoon vanilla extract, unsweetened
- ½ teaspoon salt
- ¼ cup melted coconut oil
- 1 egg, pastured
- ¼ cup applesauce, unsweetened
- ¼ cup almond milk, unsweetened

Method:

1. Switch on the air fryer, insert fryer basket, grease it with olive oil, then shut with its lid, set the fryer at 360 degrees F and preheat for 10 minutes.
2. Meanwhile, place flour in a large bowl, add berries, salt, sweetener, and baking powder and stir until well combined.
3. Crack the eggs in another bowl, whisk in vanilla, milk, and applesauce until combined and then slowly whisk in flour mixture until incorporated.
4. Take fourteen silicone muffin cups, grease them with oil, and then evenly fill them with the prepared batter.
5. Open the fryer, stack muffin cups in it, close with its lid and cook for 10 minutes until muffins are nicely golden brown and set.
6. When air fryer beeps, open its lid, transfer muffins onto a serving plate and then remaining muffins in the same manner.
7. Serve straight away.

Nutrition Value:

- Calories: 201 Cal
- Carbs: 27.3 g
- Fat: 8.8 g
- Protein: 3 g
- Fiber: 1.2 g

Baked Eggs

Preparation time: 5 minutes
Cooking time: 17 minutes
Servings: 2

Ingredients:

- 2 tablespoons frozen spinach, thawed
- ½ teaspoon salt
- ¼ teaspoon ground black pepper
- 2 eggs, pastured
- 3 teaspoons grated parmesan cheese, reduced-fat
- 2 tablespoons milk, unsweetened, reduced-fat

Method:

1. Switch on the air fryer, insert fryer basket, grease it with olive oil, then shut with its lid, set the fryer at 330 degrees F and preheat for 5 minutes.
2. Meanwhile, take two silicon muffin cups, grease them with oil, then crack an egg into each cup and evenly add cheese, spinach, and milk.
3. Season the egg with salt and black pepper and gently stir the ingredients, without breaking the egg yolk.
4. Open the fryer, add muffin cups in it, close with its lid and cook for 8 to 12 minutes until eggs have cooked to desired doneness.
5. When air fryer beeps, open its lid, take out the muffin cups and serve.

Nutrition Value:

- Calories: 161 Cal
- Carbs: 3 g
- Fat: 11.4 g
- Protein: 12.1 g
- Fiber: 1.1 g

Bagels

Preparation time: 10 minutes
Cooking time: 20 minutes
Servings: 6

Ingredients:

- 2 cups almond flour
- 2 cups shredded mozzarella cheese, low-fat
- 2 tablespoons butter, unsalted
- 1 1/2 teaspoon baking powder
- 1 teaspoon apple cider vinegar
- 1 egg, pastured

For Egg Wash:

- 1 egg, pastured
- 1 teaspoon butter, unsalted, melted

Method:

1. Place flour in a heatproof bowl, add cheese and butter, then stir well and microwave for 90 seconds until butter and cheese has melted.
2. Then stir the mixture until well combined, let it cool for 5 minutes and whisk in the egg, baking powder, and vinegar until incorporated and dough comes together.
3. Let the dough cool for 10 minutes, then divide the dough into six sections, shape each section into a bagel and let the bagels rest for 5 minutes.
4. Prepare the egg wash and for this, place the melted butter in a bowl, whisk in the egg until blended and then brush the mixture generously on top of each bagel.
5. Take a fryer basket, line it with parchment paper and then place prepared bagels in it in a single layer.
6. Switch on the air fryer, insert fryer, then shut with its lid, set the fryer at 350 degrees F and cook for 10 minutes at the 350 degrees F until bagels are nicely golden and thoroughly cooked, turning the bagels halfway through the frying.
7. When air fryer beeps, open its lid, transfer bagels to a serving plate and cook the remaining bagels in the same manner.

8. Serve straight away.

Nutrition Value:

- Calories: 408.7 Cal
- Carbs: 8.3 g
- Fat: 33.5 g
- Protein: 20.3 g
- Fiber: 4 g

Cauliflower Hash Browns

Preparation time: 10 minutes
Cooking time: 25 minutes
Servings: 6

Ingredients:

- 1/4 cup chickpea flour
- 4 cups cauliflower rice
- 1/2 medium white onion, peeled and chopped
- 1/2 teaspoon garlic powder
- 1 tablespoon xanthan gum
- 1/2 teaspoon salt
- 1 tablespoon nutritional yeast flakes
- 1 teaspoon ground paprika

Method:

1. Switch on the air fryer, insert fryer basket, grease it with olive oil, then shut with its lid, set the fryer at 375 degrees F and preheat for 10 minutes.
2. Meanwhile, place all the ingredients in a bowl, stir until well mixed and then shape the mixture into six rectangular disks, each about ½-inch thick.
3. Open the fryer, add hash browns in it in a single layer, close with its lid and cook for 25 minutes at the 375 degrees F until nicely golden and crispy, turning halfway through the frying.
4. When air fryer beeps, open its lid, transfer hash browns to a serving plate and serve.

Nutrition Value:

- Calories: 115.2 Cal
- Carbs: 6.2 g
- Fat: 7.3 g
- Protein: 7.4 g
- Fiber: 2.2 g

Cornbread

Preparation time: 10 minutes
Cooking time: 25 minutes
Servings: 8

Ingredients:

- 3/4 cup almond flour
- 1 cup white cornmeal
- 1 tablespoon erythritol sweetener
- 1 1/2 teaspoons baking powder
- 1/4 teaspoon salt
- 1/2 teaspoon baking soda
- 6 tablespoons butter, unsalted; melted
- 2 eggs; beaten
- 1 1/2 cups buttermilk, low-fat

Method:

1. Switch on the air fryer, insert fryer pan, grease it with olive oil, then shut with its lid, set the fryer at 360 degrees F and preheat for 5 minutes.
2. Meanwhile, crack the egg in a bowl and then whisk in butter and milk until blended.
3. Place flour in another bowl, add remaining ingredients, stir until well mixed and then stir in egg mixture until incorporated.
4. Open the fryer, pour the batter into the fryer pan, close with its lid and cook for 25 minutes at the 360 degrees F until nicely golden and crispy, shaking halfway through the frying.
5. When air fryer beeps, open its lid, take out the fryer pan, and then transfer the bread onto a serving plate.
6. Cut the bread into pieces and serve.

Nutrition Value:

- Calories: 138 Cal
- Carbs: 25 g
- Fat: 2 g
- Protein: 5 g
- Fiber: 2 g

Chapter 6: Poultry

Caribbean Spiced Chicken

Preparation time: 45 minutes
Cooking time: 20 minutes
Servings: 4

Ingredients:

- 1.5-pound boneless chicken thigh fillets, skinless, pastured
- ½ tablespoon ground ginger
- ¾ teaspoon ground black pepper
- ½ tablespoon ground nutmeg
- 1 teaspoon salt
- ½ tablespoon cayenne pepper
- ½ tablespoon ground coriander
- ½ tablespoon ground cinnamon
- 1½ tablespoon olive oil

Method:

1. Meanwhile, take a baking sheet, line it with paper towels, then place chicken on it, season the chicken with salt and black pepper on both sides and let it sit for 30 minutes.
2. Prepare the spice mix and for this, place remaining ingredients in a bowl, except for oil, and then stir well until mixed.
3. Pat dry the chicken, then season well with the spice mix and brush with oil.
4. Switch on the air fryer, insert fryer basket, grease it with olive oil, then shut with its lid, set the fryer at 390 degrees F and preheat for 5 minutes.
5. Then open the fryer, add seasoned chicken in it in a single layer, close with its lid and cook for 10 minutes until nicely golden and cooked, turning the chicken halfway through the frying.
6. When air fryer beeps, open its lid, transfer chicken into a heatproof dish and then cover it with foil to keep the chicken warm.
7. Cook remaining chicken in the same manner and serve.

Nutrition Value:
- Calories: 202 Cal
- Carbs: 1.7 g
- Fat: 13.4 g
- Protein: 25 g
- Fiber: 0.4 g

Chicken Sandwich

Preparation time: 40 minutes
Cooking time: 20 minutes
Servings: 6

Ingredients:

- 4 chicken breasts, pastured
- 1 cup almond flour
- ¾ teaspoon ground black pepper
- 1/2 teaspoon paprika
- 1 teaspoon salt
- 1/2 teaspoon celery seeds
- 1 teaspoon potato starch
- 1/4 cup milk, reduced-fat
- 4 cups dill pickle juice as needed
- 2 eggs, pastured
- 4 hamburger buns
- 1/8 teaspoon dry milk powder, nonfat
- ¼ teaspoon xanthan gum
- 1/8 teaspoon erythritol sweetener

Method:

1. Place the chicken in a large plastic bag, seal the bag and then pound the chicken with a mallet until ½-inch thick.
2. Brine the chicken and for this, pour the dill pickle juice in the plastic bag containing chicken, then seal it and let the chicken soak for a minimum of 2 hours.
3. After 2 hours, remove the chicken from the brine, rinse it well, and pat dry with paper towels.
4. Place flour in a shallow dish, add black pepper, paprika, salt, celery, potato starch, milk powder, xanthan gum, and sweetener and stir until well mixed.
5. Crack eggs in another dish and then whisk until blended.
6. Switch on the air fryer, insert fryer basket, grease it with olive oil, then shut with its lid, set the fryer at 375 degrees F and preheat for 5 minutes.

7. Meanwhile, dip the chicken into the egg and then coat evenly with the flour mixture.
8. Open the fryer, add chicken breasts in it in a single layer, close with its lid, then cook for 10 minutes, flip the chickens and continue cooking for 5 minutes or until chicken is nicely golden and cooked.
9. When air fryer beeps, open its lid, transfer chicken into a plate and cook remaining chicken in the same manner.
10. Sandwich a chicken breast between toasted hamburger buns, top with favorite dressing and serve.

Nutrition Value:

- Calories: 440 Cal
- Carbs: 40 g
- Fat: 19 g
- Protein: 28 g
- Fiber: 12 g

Buttermilk Fried Chicken

Preparation time: 20 minutes
Cooking time: 10 minutes
Servings: 4

Ingredients:

- 3 tablespoons cornmeal, ground
- 1-pound chicken breasts, pastured
- 6 tablespoons cornflakes
- 1 teaspoon garlic powder
- ¼ teaspoon ground black pepper
- 1 teaspoon paprika
- ¼ teaspoon salt
- ¼ teaspoon hot sauce
- 1/3 cup buttermilk, low-fat

Method:

1. Pour milk in a bowl, add hot sauce and whisk until well mixed.
2. Cut the chicken in half lengthwise into four pieces, then add into buttermilk, toss well until well coated and let it sit for 15 minutes.
3. Place cornflakes in a blender or food processor, pulse until mixture resembles crumbs, then add remaining ingredients, pulse until well mixed and then tip the mixture into a shallow dish.
4. After 15 minutes, remove chicken from the buttermilk, then coat with cornflakes mixture until evenly coated and place the chicken on a wire rack.
5. Switch on the air fryer, insert fryer basket, grease it with olive oil, then shut with its lid, set the fryer at 375 degrees F and preheat for 5 minutes.
6. Then open the fryer, add chicken in it in a single layer, spray with oil, close with its lid and cook for 10 minutes until nicely golden and cooked, turning the chicken halfway through the frying.
7. When air fryer beeps, open its lid, transfer chicken onto a serving plate and serve.

Nutrition Value:

- Calories: 160 Cal
- Carbs: 7 g
- Fat: 3.5 g
- Protein: 24 g
- Fiber: 1 g

Chicken Wings

Preparation time: 10 minutes
Cooking time: 1 hour and 30 minutes
Servings: 4

Ingredients:

- 3 pounds chicken wing parts, pastured
- 1 tablespoon old bay seasoning
- 1 teaspoon lemon zest
- 3/4 cup potato starch
- 1/2 cup butter, unsalted, melted

Method:

1. Switch on the air fryer, insert fryer basket, grease it with olive oil, then shut with its lid, set the fryer at 360 degrees F and preheat for 5 minutes.
2. Meanwhile, pat dry chicken wings and then place them in a bowl.
3. Stir together seasoning and starch, add to chicken wings and stir well until evenly coated.
4. Open the fryer, add chicken wings in it in a single layer, close with its lid and cook for 35 minutes, shaking every 10 minutes.
5. Then switch the temperature of air fryer to 400 degrees F and continue air frying the chicken wings for 10 minutes or until nicely golden brown and cooked, shaking every 3 minutes.
6. When air fryer beeps, open its lid, transfer chicken wings onto a serving plate and cook the remaining wings in the same manner.
7. Whisk together melted butter and lemon zest until blended and serve it with the chicken wings.

Nutrition Value:

- Calories: 240 Cal
- Carbs: 4 g
- Fat: 16 g
- Protein: 20 g
- Fiber: 0 g

Chicken Tenders

Preparation time: 5 minutes
Cooking time: 10 minutes
Servings: 2

Ingredients:

- 1/8 cup almond flour
- 12 ounces chicken breasts, pastured
- ½ teaspoon ground black pepper
- ¾ teaspoon salt
- 1.2 ounces panko bread crumbs
- 1 egg white, pastured

Method:

1. Switch on the air fryer, insert fryer basket, grease it with olive oil, then shut with its lid, set the fryer at 350 degrees F and preheat for 5 minutes.
2. Meanwhile, season the chicken with salt and black pepper on both sides and then evenly coat with flour.
3. Crack the egg, whisk until blended, dip the coated chicken in it and then coat with bread crumbs.
4. Open the fryer, add chicken in it, close with its lid and cook for 10 minutes until nicely golden and cooked, turning the chicken halfway through the frying.
5. When air fryer beeps, open its lid, transfer chicken onto a serving plate and serve.

Nutrition Value:

- Calories: 112 Cal
- Carbs: 7.1 g
- Fat: 6.2 g
- Protein: 7 g
- Fiber: 0.3 g

Chicken Nuggets

Preparation time: 10 minutes
Cooking time: 24 minutes
Servings: 4

Ingredients:

- 1-pound chicken breast, pastured
- 1/4 cup coconut flour
- 6 tablespoons toasted sesame seeds
- 1/2 teaspoon ginger powder
- 1/8 teaspoon sea salt
- 1 teaspoon sesame oil
- 4 egg whites, pastured

Method:

1. Switch on the air fryer, insert fryer basket, grease it with olive oil, then shut with its lid, set the fryer at 400 degrees F and preheat for 10 minutes.
2. Meanwhile, cut the chicken breast into 1-inch pieces, pat them dry, place the chicken pieces in a bowl, sprinkle with salt and oil and toss until well coated.
3. Place flour in a large plastic bag, add ginger and chicken, seal the bag and turn it upside down to coat the chicken with flour evenly.
4. Place egg whites in a bowl, whisk well, then add coated chicken and toss until well coated.
5. Place sesame seeds in a large plastic bag, add chicken pieces in it, seal the bag and turn it upside down to coat the chicken with sesame seeds evenly.
6. Open the fryer, add chicken nuggets in it in a single layer, spray with oil, close with its lid and cook for 12 minutes until nicely golden and cooked, turning the chicken nuggets and spraying with oil halfway through.
7. When air fryer beeps, open its lid, transfer chicken nuggets onto a serving plate and fry the remaining chicken nuggets in the same manner.
8. Serve straight away.

Nutrition Value:

- Calories: 312 Cal
- Carbs: 9 g
- Fat: 15 g
- Protein: 33.6 g
- Fiber: 5 g

Chicken Meatballs

Preparation time: 5 minutes
Cooking time: 26 minutes
Servings: 4

Ingredients:

- 1-pound ground chicken
- 2 green onions, chopped
- ¾ teaspoon ground black pepper
- 1/4 cup shredded coconut, unsweetened
- 1 teaspoon salt
- 1 tablespoon hoisin sauce
- 1 tablespoon soy sauce
- 1/2 cup cilantro, chopped
- 1 teaspoon Sriracha sauce
- 1 teaspoon sesame oil

Method:

1. Switch on the air fryer, insert fryer basket, grease it with olive oil, then shut with its lid, set the fryer at 350 degrees F and preheat for 5 minutes.
2. Meanwhile, place all the ingredients in a bowl, stir until well mixed and then shape the mixture into meatballs, 1 teaspoon of chicken mixture per meatball.
3. Open the fryer, add chicken meatballs in it in a single layer, close with its lid and then spray with oil.
4. Cook the chicken meatballs for 10 minutes, flipping the meatballs halfway through, and then continue cooking for 3 minutes until golden.
5. When air fryer beeps, open its lid, transfer chicken meatballs onto a serving plate and then cook the remaining meatballs in the same manner.
6. Serve straight away.

Nutrition Value:

- Calories: 223 Cal
- Carbs: 3 g
- Fat: 14 g
- Protein: 20 g
- Fiber: 1 g

Buffalo Chicken Hot Wings

Preparation time: 10 minutes
Cooking time: 45 minutes
Servings: 6

Ingredients:

- 16 chicken wings, pastured
- 1 teaspoon garlic powder
- 2 teaspoons chicken seasoning
- ¾ teaspoon ground black pepper
- 2 teaspoons soy sauce
- 1/4 cup buffalo sauce, reduced-fat

Method:

1. Switch on the air fryer, insert fryer basket, grease it with olive oil, then shut with its lid, set the fryer at 400 degrees F and preheat for 5 minutes.
2. Meanwhile, place chicken wings in a bowl, drizzle with soy sauce, toss until well coated and then season with black pepper and garlic powder.
3. Open the fryer, stack chicken wings in it, then spray with oil and close with its lid.
4. Cook the chicken wings for 10 minutes, turning the wings halfway through, and then transfer them to a bowl, covering the bowl with a foil to keep the chicken wings warm.
5. Air fry the remaining chicken wings in the same manner, then transfer them to the bowl, add buffalo sauce and toss until well coated.
6. Return chicken wings into the fryer basket in a single layer and continue frying for 7 to 12 minutes or until chicken wings are glazed and crispy, shaking the chicken wings every 3 to 4 minutes.
7. Serve straight away.

Nutrition Value:

- Calories: 88 Cal
- Carbs: 2.6 g
- Fat: 6.5 g
- Protein: 4.5 g
- Fiber: 0.1 g

Herb Chicken Thighs

Preparation time: 6 hours and 25 minutes
Cooking time: 40 minutes
Servings: 6

Ingredients:

- 6 chicken thighs, skin-on, pastured
- 2 teaspoons garlic powder
- 1/2 teaspoon onion powder
- 1 teaspoon dried basil
- 1 teaspoon spike seasoning
- 1/2 teaspoon dried sage
- 1/4 teaspoon ground black pepper
- 1/2 teaspoon dried oregano
- 2 tablespoons lemon juice
- 1/4 cup olive oil

Method:

1. Prepare the marinade and for this, place all the ingredients in a bowl, except for chicken, stir until well combined and then pour the marinade in a large plastic bag.
2. Add chicken thighs in the plastic bag, seal the bag, then turn in upside down until chicken thighs are coated with the marinade and let marinate in the refrigerator for minimum of 6 hours.
3. Then drain the chicken, arrange the chicken thighs on a wire rack and let them rest for 15 minutes at room temperature.
4. Meanwhile, switch on the air fryer, insert fryer basket, grease it with olive oil, then shut with its lid, set the fryer at 360 degrees F and preheat for 5 minutes.
5. Then open the fryer, add chicken thighs in it in a single layer top-side down, close with its lid, cook the chicken for 8 minutes, turn the chicken, and continue frying for 6 minutes.
6. Turn the chicken thighs and then continue cooking for another 6 minutes or until chicken is nicely browned and cooked.

7. When air fryer beeps, open its lid, transfer chicken onto a serving plate and cook the remaining chicken thighs in the same manner.
8. Serve straight away.

Nutrition Value:

- Calories: 163 Cal
- Carbs: 1 g
- Fat: 9.2 g
- Protein: 19.4 g
- Fiber: 0.3 g

Lemon Pepper Chicken

Preparation time: 1 hour and 10 minutes
Cooking time: 28 minutes
Servings: 4

Ingredients:

- 4 chicken breasts, pastured
- 1/4 cup lemon juice
- 3 tablespoon lemon pepper seasoning
- 2 teaspoons Worcestershire sauce
- 1/4 cup olive oil

Method:

1. Prepare the marinade and for this, place oil, Worcestershire sauce, salt and lemon juice in a bowl and whisk until combined.
2. Cut each chicken breast into four pieces, add the chicken pieces into the marinade, toss until well coated and marinate the chicken in the refrigerator for a minimum of 1 hour.
3. Then switch on the air fryer, insert fryer basket, grease it with olive oil, then shut with its lid, set the fryer at 350 degrees F and preheat for 5 minutes.
4. Open the fryer, add chicken pieces in it in a single layer, spray with oil, close with its lid and cook for 14 minutes at the 350 degrees F until nicely golden and cooked, turning the chicken halfway through the frying.
5. When air fryer beeps, open its lid, transfer chicken onto a serving plate and cook the remaining chicken pieces in the same manner.
6. Serve straight away.

Nutrition Value:

- Calories: 55 Cal
- Carbs: 1.3 g
- Fat: 2.7 g
- Protein: 6.6 g
- Fiber: 0.5 g

Chapter 7: Appetizers and Siders

Ravioli

Preparation time: 5 minutes
Cooking time: 16 minutes
Servings: 4

Ingredients:

- 8 ounces frozen vegan ravioli, thawed
- 1 teaspoon dried basil
- 1 teaspoon garlic powder
- 1/8 teaspoon ground black pepper
- ¼ teaspoon salt
- 1 teaspoon dried oregano
- 2 teaspoons nutritional yeast flakes
- 1/2 cup marinara sauce, unsweetened
- 1/2 cup panko bread crumbs
- 1/4 cup liquid from chickpeas can

Method:

1. Place breadcrumbs in a bowl, sprinkle with salt, basil, oregano, and black pepper, add garlic powder and yeast and stir until mixed.
2. Take a bowl and then pour in chickpeas liquid in it.
3. Working on one ravioli at a time, first dip a ravioli in chickpeas liquid and then coat with breadcrumbs mixture.
4. Prepare remaining ravioli in the same manner, then take a fryer basket, grease it well with oil and place ravioli in it in a single layer.
5. Switch on the air fryer, insert fryer basket, sprinkle oil on ravioli, shut with its lid, set the fryer at 390 degrees F, then cook for 6 minutes, turn the ravioli and continue cooking 2 minutes until nicely golden and heated thoroughly.
6. Cook the remaining ravioli in the same manner and serve with marinara sauce.

Nutrition Value:

- Calories: 150 Cal
- Carbs: 27 g
- Fat: 3 g
- Protein: 5 g
- Fiber: 2 g

Onion Rings

Preparation time: 10 minutes
Cooking time: 32 minutes
Servings: 4

Ingredients:

- 1 large white onion, peeled
- 2/3 cup pork rinds
- 3 tablespoons almond flour
- 1/2 teaspoon garlic powder
- 1/2 teaspoon paprika
- 1/4 teaspoon sea salt
- 3 tablespoons coconut flour
- 2 eggs, pastured

Method:

1. Switch on the air fryer, insert fryer basket, grease it with olive oil, then shut with its lid, set the fryer at 400 degrees F and preheat for 10 minutes.
2. Meanwhile, slice the peeled onion into ½ inch thick rings.
3. Take a shallow dish, add almond flour and stir in garlic powder, paprika, and pork rinds; take another shallow dish, add coconut flour and salt and stir until mixed.
4. Crack eggs in a bowl and then whisk until combined.
5. Working on one onion ring at a time, first coat onion ring in coconut flour mixture, then it in egg, and coat with pork rind mixture by scooping over the onion until evenly coated.
6. Open the fryer, place coated onion rings in it in a single layer, spray oil over onion rings, close with its lid and cook for 16 minutes until nicely golden and thoroughly cooked, flipping the onion rings halfway through the frying.
7. When air fryer beeps, open its lid, transfer onion rings onto a serving plate and cook the remaining onion rings in the same manner.
8. Serve straight away.

Nutrition Value:

- Calories: 135 Cal
- Carbs: 8 g
- Fat: 7 g
- Protein: 8 g
- Fiber: 3 g

Cauliflower Fritters

Preparation time: 10 minutes
Cooking time: 14 minutes
Servings: 2

Ingredients:

- 5 cups chopped cauliflower florets
- 1/2 cup almond flour
- 1/2 teaspoon baking powder
- ½ teaspoon ground black pepper
- ½ teaspoon salt
- 2 eggs, pastured

Method:

1. Add chopped cauliflower in a blender or food processor, pulse until minced and then tip the mixture in a bowl.
2. Add remaining ingredients, stir well and then shape the mixture into 1/3-inch patties, an ice cream scoop of mixture per patty.
3. Switch on the air fryer, insert fryer basket, grease it with olive oil, then shut with its lid, set the fryer at 390 degrees F and preheat for 5 minutes.
4. Then open the fryer, add cauliflower patties in it in a single layer, spray oil over patties, close with its lid and cook for 14 minutes at the 375 degrees F until nicely golden and cooked, flipping the patties halfway through the frying.
5. Serve straight away with the dip.

Nutrition Value:

- Calories: 272 Cal
- Carbs: 57 g
- Fat: 0.3 g
- Protein: 11 g
- Fiber: 8 g

Zucchini Fritters

Preparation time: 20 minutes
Cooking time: 12 minutes
Servings: 4

Ingredients:

- 2 medium zucchinis, ends trimmed
- 3 tablespoons almond flour
- 1 tablespoon salt
- 1 teaspoon garlic powder
- ¼ teaspoon paprika
- ¼ teaspoon ground black pepper
- ¼ teaspoon onion powder
- 1 egg, pastured

Method:

1. Wash and pat dry the zucchini, then cut its ends and grate the zucchini.
2. Place grated zucchini in a colander, sprinkle with salt and let it rest for 10 minutes.
3. Then wrap zucchini in a kitchen cloth and squeeze moisture from it as much as possible and place dried zucchini in another bowl.
4. Add remaining ingredients into the zucchini and then stir until mixed.
5. Take fryer basket, line it with parchment paper, grease it with oil and drop zucchini mixture on it by a spoonful, about 1-inch apart and then spray well with oil.
6. Switch on the air fryer, insert fryer basket, then shut with its lid, set the fryer at 360 degrees F and cook the fritter for 12 minutes until nicely golden and cooked, flipping the fritters halfway through the frying.
7. Serve straight away.

Nutrition Value:

- Calories: 57 Cal
- Carbs: 8 g
- Fat: 1 g
- Protein: 3 g
- Fiber: 1 g

Kale Chips

Preparation time: 5 minutes
Cooking time: 7 minutes
Servings: 2

Ingredients:

- 1 large bunch of kale
- ¾ teaspoon red chili powder
- 1 teaspoon salt
- ¾ teaspoon ground black pepper

Method:

1. Remove the hard spines form the kale leaves, then cut kale into small pieces and place them in a fryer basket.
2. Spray oil over kale, then sprinkle with salt, chili powder and black pepper and toss until well mixed.
3. Switch on the air fryer, insert fryer basket, then shut with its lid, set the fryer at 375 degrees F and cook for 7 minutes until kale is crispy, shaking halfway through the frying.
4. When air fryer beeps, open its lid, transfer kale chips onto a serving plate and serve.

Nutrition Value:

- Calories: 66.2 Cal
- Carbs: 7.3 g
- Fat: 4 g
- Protein: 2.5 g
- Fiber: 2.6 g

Radish Chips

Preparation time: 5 minutes
Cooking time: 20 minutes
Servings: 2

Ingredients:

- 8 ounces radish slices
- ½ teaspoon garlic powder
- 1 teaspoon salt
- ½ teaspoon onion powder
- ½ teaspoon ground black pepper

Method:

1. Wash the radish slices, pat them dry, place them in a fryer basket, and then spray oil on them until well coated.
2. Sprinkle salt, garlic powder, onion powder, and black pepper over radish slices and then toss until well coated.
3. Switch on the air fryer, insert fryer basket, then shut with its lid, set the fryer at 370 degrees F and cook for 10 minutes, stirring the slices halfway through.
4. Then spray oil on radish slices, shake the basket and continue frying for 10 minutes, stirring the chips halfway through.
5. Serve straight away.

Nutrition Value:

- Calories: 21 Cal
- Carbs: 1 g
- Fat: 1.8 g
- Protein: 0.2 g
- Fiber: 0.4 g

Zucchini Fries

Preparation time: 10 minutes
Cooking time: 20 minutes
Servings: 4

Ingredients:

- 2 medium zucchinis
- ½ cup almond flour
- 1/8 teaspoon ground black pepper
- ½ teaspoon garlic powder
- 1/8 teaspoon salt
- 1 teaspoon Italian seasoning
- ½ cup grated parmesan cheese, reduced-fat
- 1 egg, pastured, beaten

Method:

1. Switch on the air fryer, insert fryer basket, grease it with olive oil, then shut with its lid, set the fryer at 400 degrees F and preheat for 10 minutes.
2. Meanwhile, cut each zucchini in half and then cut each zucchini half into 4-inch-long pieces, each about ½-inch thick.
3. Place flour in a shallow dish, add remaining ingredients except for the egg and stir until mixed.
4. Crack the egg in a bowl and then whisk until blended.
5. Working on one zucchini piece at a time, first dip it in the egg, then coat it in the almond flour mixture and place it on a wire rack.
6. Open the fryer, add zucchini pieces in it in a single layer, spray oil over zucchini, close with its lid and cook for 10 minutes until nicely golden and crispy, shaking halfway through the frying.
7. Cook remaining zucchini pieces in the same manner and serve.

Nutrition Value:

- Calories: 147 Cal
- Carbs: 6 g
- Fat: 10 g
- Protein: 9 g
- Fiber: 2 g

Avocado fries

Preparation time: 10 minutes
Cooking time: 20 minutes
Servings: 2

Ingredients:

- 1 medium avocado, pitted
- 1 egg
- 1/2 cup almond flour
- ¼ teaspoon salt
- ¼ teaspoon ground black pepper
- 1/2 teaspoon salt

Method:

1. Switch on the air fryer, insert fryer basket, grease it with olive oil, then shut with its lid, set the fryer at 400 degrees F and preheat for 10 minutes.
2. Meanwhile, cut the avocado in half and then cut each half into wedges, each about ½-inch thick.
3. Place flour in a shallow dish, add salt and black pepper and stir until mixed.
4. Crack the egg in a bowl and then whisk until blended.
5. Working on one avocado piece at a time, first dip it in the egg, then coat it in the almond flour mixture and place it on a wire rack.
6. Open the fryer, add avocado pieces in it in a single layer, spray oil over avocado, close with its lid and cook for 10 minutes until nicely golden and crispy, shaking halfway through the frying.
7. When air fryer beeps, open its lid, transfer avocado fries onto a serving plate and serve.

Nutrition Value:

- Calories: 251 Cal
- Carbs: 19 g
- Fat: 17 g
- Protein: 6 g
- Fiber: 7 g

Roasted Peanut Butter Squash

Preparation time: 5 minutes
Cooking time: 22 minutes
Servings: 4

Ingredients:

- 1 butternut squash, peeled
- 1 teaspoon cinnamon
- 1 tablespoon olive oil

Method:

1. Switch on the air fryer, insert fryer basket, grease it with olive oil, then shut with its lid, set the fryer at 220 degrees F and preheat for 5 minutes.
2. Meanwhile, peel the squash400 cut it into 1-inch pieces, and then place them in a bowl.
3. Drizzle oil over squash pieces, sprinkle with cinnamon and then toss until well coated.
4. Open the fryer, add squash pieces in it, close with its lid and cook for 17 minutes until nicely golden and crispy, shaking every 5 minutes.
5. When air fryer beeps, open its lid, transfer squash onto a serving plate and serve.

Nutrition Value:

- Calories: 116 Cal
- Carbs: 22 g
- Fat: 3 g
- Protein: 1 g
- Fiber: 4 g

Roasted Chickpeas

Preparation time: 35 minutes
Cooking time: 25 minutes
Servings: 6

Ingredients:

- 15-ounce cooked chickpeas
- 1 teaspoon garlic powder
- 1 tablespoon nutritional yeast
- 1/8 teaspoon cumin
- 1 teaspoon smoked paprika
- 1/2 teaspoon salt
- 1 tablespoon olive oil

Method:

1. Take a large baking sheet, line it with paper towels, then spread chickpeas on it, cover the peas with paper towels, and let rest for 30 minutes or until chickpeas are dried.
2. Then switch on the air fryer, insert fryer basket, grease it with olive oil, then shut with its lid, set the fryer at 355 degrees F and preheat for 5 minutes.
3. Place dried chickpeas in a bowl, add remaining ingredients and toss until well coated.
4. Open the fryer, add chickpeas in it, close with its lid and cook for 20 minutes until nicely golden and crispy, shaking the chickpeas every 5 minutes.
5. When air fryer beeps, open its lid, transfer chickpeas onto a serving bowl and serve.

Nutrition Value:

- Calories: 124 Cal
- Carbs: 17.4 g
- Fat: 4.4 g
- Protein: 4.7 g
- Fiber: 4 g

Chapter 8: Beef, Pork and Lamb

Pork Chops

Preparation time: 5 minutes
Cooking time: 15 minutes
Servings: 5

Ingredients:

- 4 slices of almond bread
- 5 pork chops, bone-in, pastured
- 3.5 ounces coconut flour
- 1 teaspoon salt
- 3 tablespoons parsley
- ½ teaspoon ground black pepper
- 1 tablespoon pork seasoning
- 2 tablespoons olive oil
- 1/3 cup apple juice, unsweetened
- 1 egg, pastured

Method:

1. Switch on the air fryer, insert fryer basket, grease it with olive oil, then shut with its lid, set the fryer at 350 degrees F and preheat for 5 minutes.
2. Meanwhile, place bread slices in a food processor and pulse until mixture resembles crumbs.
3. Tip the bread crumbs in a shallow dish, add parsley, ½ teaspoon salt, ¼ teaspoon ground black pepper and stir until mixed.
4. Place flour in another shallow dish, add remaining salt and black pepper, along with pork seasoning and stir until mixed.
5. Crack the egg in a bowl, pour in apple juice and whisk until combined.
6. Working on one pork chop at a time, first coat it into the flour mixture, then dip into egg and then evenly coat with breadcrumbs mixture.

7. Open the fryer, add coated pork chops in it in a single layer, close with its lid and cook for 10 minutes until nicely golden and cooked, flipping the pork chops halfway through the frying.
8. When air fryer beeps, open its lid, transfer pork chops onto a serving plate and serve.

Nutrition Value:

- Calories: 441 Cal
- Carbs: 28.6 g
- Fat: 22.3 g
- Protein: 30.6 g
- Fiber: 0.5 g

Steak

Preparation time: 10 minutes
Cooking time: 18 minutes
Servings: 2

Ingredients:

- 2 steaks, grass-fed, each about 6 ounces and ¾ inch thick
- 1 tablespoon butter, unsalted
- ¾ teaspoon ground black pepper
- 1/2 teaspoon garlic powder
- ¾ teaspoon salt
- 1 teaspoon olive oil

Method:

1. Switch on the air fryer, insert fryer basket, grease it with olive oil, then shut with its lid, set the fryer at 400 degrees F and preheat for 5 minutes.
2. Meanwhile, coat the steaks with oil and then season with black pepper, garlic, and salt.
3. Open the fryer, add steaks in it, close with its lid and cook 10 to 18 minutes at until nicely golden and steaks are cooked to desired doneness, flipping the steaks halfway through the frying.
4. When air fryer beeps, open its lid and transfer steaks to a cutting board.
5. Take two large pieces of aluminum foil, place a steak on each piece, top steak with ½ tablespoon butter, then cover with foil and let it rest for 5 minutes.
6. Serve straight away.

Nutrition Value:

- Calories: 82 Cal
- Carbs: 0 g
- Fat: 5 g
- Protein: 8.7 g
- Fiber: 0 g

Meatloaf Slider Wraps

Preparation time: 15 minutes
Cooking time: 10 minutes
Servings: 6

Ingredients:

- 1-pound ground beef, grass-fed
- ½ cup almond flour
- ¼ cup coconut flour
- ½ tablespoon minced garlic
- ¼ cup chopped white onion
- 1 teaspoon Italian seasoning
- ½ teaspoon sea salt
- ½ teaspoon dried tarragon
- ½ teaspoon ground black pepper
- 1 tablespoon Worcestershire sauce
- ¼ cup ketchup
- 2 eggs, pastured, beaten

Method:

1. Place all the ingredients in a bowl, stir well, then shape the mixture into 2-inch diameter and 1-inch thick patties and refrigerate them for 10 minutes.
2. Meanwhile, switch on the air fryer, insert fryer basket, grease it with olive oil, then shut with its lid, set the fryer at 360 degrees F and preheat for 10 minutes.
3. Open the fryer, add patties in it in a single layer, close with its lid and cook for 10 minutes until nicely golden and cooked, flipping the patties halfway through the frying.
4. When air fryer beeps, open its lid and transfer patties to a plate.
5. Wrap each patty in lettuce and serve.

Nutrition Value:

- Calories: 228 Cal
- Carbs: 6 g
- Fat: 16 g
- Protein: 13 g
- Fiber: 2 g

Pork Belly

Preparation time: 20 minutes
Cooking time: 40 minutes
Servings: 4

Ingredients:

- 1-pound pork belly, pastured
- 6 cloves of garlic, peeled
- 1 teaspoon ground black pepper
- 1 teaspoon salt
- 2 tablespoons soy sauce
- 2 bay leaves
- 3 cups of water

Method:

1. Cut the pork belly evenly into three pieces, place them in an instant pot, and add remaining ingredients.
2. Switch on the instant pot, then shut it with lid and cook the pork belly for 15 minutes at high pressure.
3. When done, let the pressure release naturally for 10 minutes and then do quick pressure release.
4. Rake out the pork by tongs and let it drain and dry for 10 minutes.
5. Then switch on the air fryer, insert fryer basket, grease it with olive oil, then shut with its lid, set the fryer at 400 degrees F and preheat for 5 minutes.
6. While the air fryer preheats, cut each piece of the pork into two long slices.
7. Open the fryer, add pork slices in it, close with its lid and cook for 15 minutes until nicely golden and crispy, flipping the pork halfway through the frying.
8. When air fryer beeps, open its lid, transfer pork slices onto a serving plate and serve.

Nutrition Value:

- Calories: 594 Cal
- Carbs: 2 g
- Fat: 60 g
- Protein: 11 g
- Fiber: 0 g

Sirloin Steak

Preparation time: 5 minutes
Cooking time: 15 minutes
Servings: 6

Ingredients:

- 2 sirloin steaks, grass-fed
- 1 tablespoon olive oil
- 2 tablespoons steak seasoning

Method:

1. Switch on the air fryer, insert fryer basket, grease it with olive oil, then shut with its lid, set the fryer at 392 degrees F and preheat for 5 minutes.
2. Meanwhile, pat dries the steaks, then brush with oil and then season well with steak seasoning until coated on both sides.
3. Open the fryer, add steaks in it, close with its lid and cook for 10 minutes until nicely golden and crispy, flipping the steaks halfway through the frying.
4. When air fryer beeps, open its lid, transfer steaks onto a serving plate and serve.

Nutrition Value:

- Calories: 253.6 Cal
- Carbs: 0.2 g
- Fat: 18.1 g
- Protein: 21.1 g
- Fiber: 0.1 g

Vietnamese Grilled Pork

Preparation time: 1 hour and 5 minutes
Cooking time: 15 minutes
Servings: 6

Ingredients:

- 1-pound sliced pork shoulder, pastured, fat trimmed
- 2 tablespoons chopped parsley
- 1/4 cup crushed roasted peanuts

For the Marinade:

- 1/4 cup minced white onions
- 1 tablespoon minced garlic
- 1 tablespoon lemongrass paste
- 1 tablespoon erythritol sweetener
- 1/2 teaspoon ground black pepper
- 1 tablespoon fish sauce
- 2 teaspoons soy sauce
- 2 tablespoons olive oil

Method:

1. Place all the ingredients for the marinade in a bowl, stir well until combined and add it into a large plastic bag.
2. Cut the pork into ½-inch slices, cut each slice into 1-inches pieces, then add them into the plastic bag containing marinade, seal the bag, turn it upside down to coat the pork pieces with the marinade and marinate for a minimum of 1 hour.
3. Then switch on the air fryer, insert fryer basket, grease it with olive oil, then shut with its lid, set the fryer at 400 degrees F and preheat for 5 minutes.
4. Open the fryer, add marinated pork in it in a single layer, close with its lid and cook for 10 minutes until nicely golden and cooked, flipping the pork halfway through the frying.
5. When air fryer beeps, open its lid, transfer pork onto a serving plate, and keep warm.

6. Air fryer the remaining pork pieces in the same manner and then serve.

Nutrition Value:

- Calories: 231 Cal
- Carbs: 4 g
- Fat: 16 g
- Protein: 16 g
- Fiber: 1 g

Meatloaf

Preparation time: 5 minutes
Cooking time: 20 minutes
Servings: 4

Ingredients:

- 1-pound ground beef, grass-fed
- 1 tablespoon minced garlic
- 1 cup white onion, peeled and diced
- 1 tablespoon minced ginger
- 1/4 cup chopped cilantro
- 2 teaspoons garam masala
- 1 teaspoon cayenne pepper
- 1 teaspoon salt
- 1/2 teaspoon ground cinnamon
- 1 teaspoon turmeric powder
- 1/8 teaspoon ground cardamom
- 2 eggs, pastured

Method:

1. Switch on the air fryer, insert fryer basket, then shut with its lid, set the fryer at 360 degrees F and preheat for 5 minutes.
2. Meanwhile, place all the ingredients in a bowl, stir until well mixed, then take an 8-inches round pan, grease it with oil, add the beef mixture in it and spread it evenly.
3. Open the fryer, place the pan in it, close with its lid and cook for 15 minutes until the top is nicely golden and meatloaf is thoroughly cooked.
4. When air fryer beeps, open its lid, take out the pan, then drain the excess fat and take out the meatloaf.
5. Cut the meatloaf into four pieces and serve.

Nutrition Value:

- Calories: 260 Cal
- Carbs: 6 g
- Fat: 13 g
- Protein: 26 g
- Fiber: 1 g

Herbed Lamb Chops

Preparation time: 1 hour and 10 minutes
Cooking time: 13 minutes
Servings: 6

Ingredients:

- 1-pound lamb chops, pastured

For the Marinate:

- 2 tablespoons lemon juice
- 1 teaspoon dried rosemary
- 1 teaspoon salt
- 1 teaspoon dried thyme
- 1 teaspoon coriander
- 1 teaspoon dried oregano
- 2 tablespoons olive oil

Method:

1. Prepare the marinade and for this, place all its ingredients in a bowl and whisk until combined.
2. Pour the marinade in a large plastic bag, add lamb chops in it, seal the bag, then turn it upside down to coat lamb chops with the marinade and let it marinate in the refrigerator for a minimum of 1 hour.
3. Then switch on the air fryer, insert fryer basket, grease it with olive oil, then shut with its lid, set the fryer at 390 degrees F and preheat for 5 minutes.
4. Meanwhile,
5. Open the fryer, add marinated lamb chops in it, close with its lid and cook for 8 minutes until nicely golden and cooked, turning the lamb chops halfway through the frying.
6. When air fryer beeps, open its lid, transfer lamb chops onto a serving plate and serve.

Nutrition Value:

- Calories: 177.4 Cal
- Carbs: 1.7 g
- Fat: 8 g
- Protein: 23.4 g
- Fiber: 0.5 g

Spicy Lamb Sirloin Steak

Preparation time: 40 minutes
Cooking time: 20 minutes
Servings: 4

Ingredients:

- 1-pound lamb sirloin steaks, pastured, boneless

For the Marinade:

- ½ of white onion, peeled
- 1 teaspoon ground fennel
- 5 cloves of garlic, peeled
- 4 slices of ginger
- 1 teaspoon salt
- 1/2 teaspoon ground cardamom
- 1 teaspoon garam masala
- 1 teaspoon ground cinnamon
- 1 teaspoon cayenne pepper

Method:

1. Place all the ingredients for the marinade in a food processor and then pulse until well blended.
2. Make cuts in the lamb chops by using a knife, then place them in a large bowl and add prepared marinade in it.
3. Mix well until lamb chops are coated with the marinade and let them marinate in the refrigerator for a minimum of 30 minutes.
4. Then switch on the air fryer, insert fryer basket, grease it with olive oil, then shut with its lid, set the fryer at 330 degrees F and preheat for 5 minutes.
5. Open the fryer, add lamb chops in it, close with its lid and cook for 15 minutes until nicely golden and cooked, flipping the steaks halfway through the frying.
6. When air fryer beeps, open its lid, transfer lamb steaks onto a serving plate and serve.

Nutrition Value:

- Calories: 182 Cal
- Carbs: 3 g
- Fat: 7 g
- Protein: 24 g
- Fiber: 1 g

Garlic Rosemary Lamb Chops

Preparation time: 1 hour and 10 minutes
Cooking time: 12 minutes
Servings: 4

Ingredients:

- 4 lamb chops, pastured
- 1 teaspoon ground black pepper
- 2 teaspoons minced garlic
- 1 ½ teaspoon salt
- 2 teaspoons olive oil
- 4 cloves of garlic, peeled
- 4 rosemary sprigs

Method:

1. Take the fryer pan, place lamb chops in it, season the top with ½ teaspoon black pepper and ¾ teaspoon salt, then drizzle evenly with oil and spread with 1 teaspoon minced garlic.
2. Add garlic cloves and rosemary and then let the lamb chops marinate in the pan into the refrigerator for a minimum of 1 hour.
3. Then switch on the air fryer, insert fryer pan, then shut with its lid, set the fryer at 360 degrees F and cook for 6 minutes.
4. Flip the lamb chops, season them with remaining salt and black pepper, add remaining minced garlic and continue cooking for 6 minutes or until lamb chops are cooked.
5. When air fryer beeps, open its lid, transfer lamb chops onto a serving plate and serve.

Nutrition Value:

- Calories: 616 Cal
- Carbs: 1 g
- Fat: 28 g
- Protein: 83 g
- Fiber: 0.3 g

Double Cheeseburger

Preparation time: 5 minutes
Cooking time: 18 minutes
Servings: 1

Ingredients:

- 2 beef patties, pastured
- 1/8 teaspoon onion powder
- 2 slices of mozzarella cheese, low fat
- 1/8 teaspoon ground black pepper
- 1/8 teaspoon salt

Method:

1. Switch on the air fryer, insert fryer basket, grease it with olive oil, then shut with its lid, set the fryer at 370 degrees F and preheat for 5 minutes.
2. Meanwhile, season the patties well with onion powder, black pepper, and salt.
3. Open the fryer, add beef patties in it, close with its lid and cook for 12 minutes until nicely golden and cooked, flipping the patties halfway through the frying.
4. Then top the patties with a cheese slice and continue cooking for 1 minute or until cheese melts.
5. Serve straight away.

Nutrition Value:

- Calories: 670 Cal
- Carbs: 0 g
- Fat: 50 g
- Protein: 39 g
- Fiber: 0 g

Steak Bites with Mushrooms

Preparation time: 5 minutes
Cooking time: 23 minutes
Servings: 3

Ingredients:

- 1-pound sirloin steaks, grass-fed
- 1/2 teaspoon garlic powder
- 8 ounces mushrooms, halved
- ¾ teaspoon ground black pepper
- 1 teaspoon Worcestershire sauce
- 1 teaspoon salt
- 2 tablespoons olive oil
- 1 teaspoon minced parsley

Method:

1. Switch on the air fryer, insert fryer basket, grease it with olive oil, then shut with its lid, set the fryer at 400 degrees F and preheat for 5 minutes.
2. Meanwhile, cut the steaks into 1-inch pieces, then add them in a bowl, add remaining ingredients except for parsley and toss until well coated.
3. Open the fryer, add steaks and mushrooms in it in a single layer, close with its lid and cook for 10 to 18 minutes or until steaks and mushrooms are cooked to desired doneness, stirring and shaking the basket halfway through the frying.
4. When air fryer beeps, open its lid, transfer steaks and mushrooms onto a serving plate and keep warm.
5. Cook remaining steaks and mushroom in the same manner, then garnish with parsley and serve.

Nutrition Value:

- Calories: 330 Cal
- Carbs: 3 g
- Fat: 21 g
- Protein: 32 g
- Fiber: 1 g

Chapter 9: Vegetarian

Cabbage Wedges

Preparation time: 10 minutes
Cooking time: 29 minutes
Servings: 6

Ingredients:

- 1 small head of green cabbage
- 6 strips of bacon, thick-cut, pastured
- 1 teaspoon onion powder
- ½ teaspoon ground black pepper
- 1 teaspoon garlic powder
- ¾ teaspoon salt
- 1/4 teaspoon red chili flakes
- 1/2 teaspoon fennel seeds
- 3 tablespoons olive oil

Method:

1. Switch on the air fryer, insert fryer basket, grease it with olive oil, then shut with its lid, set the fryer at 350 degrees F and preheat for 5 minutes.
2. Open the fryer, add bacon strips in it, close with its lid and cook for 10 minutes until nicely golden and crispy, turning the bacon halfway through the frying.
3. Meanwhile, prepare the cabbage and for this, remove the outer leaves of the cabbage and then cut it into eight wedges, keeping the core intact.
4. Prepare the spice mix and for this, place onion powder in a bowl, add black pepper, garlic powder, salt, red chili, and fennel and stir until mixed.
5. Drizzle cabbage wedges with oil and then sprinkle with spice mix until well coated.
6. When air fryer beeps, open its lid, transfer bacon strips to a cutting board and let it rest.
7. Add seasoned cabbage wedges into the fryer basket, close with its lid, then cook for 8 minutes at 400 degrees F, flip the cabbage, spray with oil and continue air frying for 6 minutes until nicely golden and cooked.

8. When done, transfer cabbage wedges to a plate.
9. Chop the bacon, sprinkle it over cabbage and serve.

Nutrition Value:

- Calories: 123 Cal
- Carbs: 2 g
- Fat: 11 g
- Protein: 4 g
- Fiber: 0 g

Buffalo Cauliflower Wings

Preparation time: 5 minutes
Cooking time: 30 minutes
Servings: 6

Ingredients:

- 1 tablespoon almond flour
- 1 medium head of cauliflower
- 1 ½ teaspoon salt
- 4 tablespoons hot sauce
- 1 tablespoon olive oil

Method:

1. Switch on the air fryer, insert fryer basket, grease it with olive oil, then shut with its lid, set the fryer at 400 degrees F and preheat for 5 minutes.
2. Meanwhile, cut cauliflower into bite-size florets and set aside.
3. Place flour in a large bowl, whisk in salt, oil and hot sauce until combined, add cauliflower florets and toss until combined.
4. Open the fryer, add cauliflower florets in it in a single layer, close with its lid and cook for 15 minutes until nicely golden and crispy, shaking halfway through the frying.
5. When air fryer beeps, open its lid, transfer cauliflower florets onto a serving plate and keep warm.
6. Cook the remaining cauliflower florets in the same manner and serve.

Nutrition Value:

- Calories: 48 Cal
- Carbs: 1 g
- Fat: 4 g
- Protein: 1 g
- Fiber: 0.5 g

Sweet Potato Cauliflower Patties

Preparation time: 20 minutes
Cooking time: 40 minutes
Servings: 7

Ingredients:

- 1 green onion, chopped
- 1 large sweet potato, peeled
- 1 teaspoon minced garlic
- 1 cup cilantro leaves
- 2 cup cauliflower florets
- ¼ teaspoon ground black pepper
- 1/4 teaspoon salt
- 1/4 cup sunflower seeds
- 1/4 teaspoon cumin
- 1/4 cup ground flaxseed
- 1/2 teaspoon red chili powder
- 2 tablespoons ranch seasoning mix
- 2 tablespoons arrowroot starch

Method:

1. Cut peeled sweet potato into small pieces, then place them in a food processor and pulse until pieces are broken up.
2. Then add onion, cauliflower florets, and garlic, pulse until combined, add remaining ingredients and pulse more until incorporated.
3. Tip the mixture in a bowl, shape the mixture into seven 1 ½ inch thick patties, each about ¼ cup, then place them on a baking sheet and freeze for 10 minutes.
4. Switch on the air fryer, insert fryer basket, grease it with olive oil, then shut with its lid, set the fryer at 400 degrees F and preheat for 10 minutes.
5. Open the fryer, add patties in it in a single layer, close with its lid and cook for 20 minutes until nicely golden and cooked, flipping the patties halfway through the frying.

6. When air fryer beeps, open its lid, transfer patties onto a serving plate and keep them warm.
7. Cook the remaining patties in the same manner and serve.

Nutrition Value:

- Calories: 85 Cal
- Carbs: 9 g
- Fat: 3 g
- Protein: 2.7 g
- Fiber: 3.5 g

Okra

Preparation time: 10 minutes
Cooking time: 10 minutes
Servings: 4

Ingredients:

- 1 cup almond flour
- 8 ounces fresh okra
- 1/2 teaspoon sea salt
- 1 cup milk, reduced-fat
- 1 egg, pastured

Method:

1. Crack the egg in a bowl, pour in the milk and whisk until blended.
2. Cut the stem from each okra, then cut it into ½-inch pieces, add them into egg and stir until well coated.
3. Mix flour and salt and add it into a large plastic bag.
4. Working on one okra piece at a time, drain the okra well by letting excess egg drip off, add it to the flour mixture, then seal the bag and shake well until okra is well coated.
5. Place the coated okra on a grease air fryer basket, coat remaining okra pieces in the same manner and place them into the basket.
6. Switch on the air fryer, insert fryer basket, spray okra with oil, then shut with its lid, set the fryer at 390 degrees F and cook for 10 minutes until nicely golden and cooked, stirring okra halfway through the frying.
7. Serve straight away.

Nutrition Value:

- Calories: 250 Cal
- Carbs: 38 g
- Fat: 9 g
- Protein: 3 g
- Fiber: 2 g

Creamed Spinach

Preparation time: 10 minutes
Cooking time: 20 minutes
Servings: 2

Ingredients:

- 1/2 cup chopped white onion
- 10 ounces frozen spinach, thawed
- 1 teaspoon salt
- 1 teaspoon ground black pepper
- 2 teaspoons minced garlic
- 1/2 teaspoon ground nutmeg
- 4 ounces cream cheese, reduced-fat, diced
- 1/4 cup shredded parmesan cheese, reduced-fat

Method:

1. Switch on the air fryer, insert fryer basket, grease it with olive oil, then shut with its lid, set the fryer at 350 degrees F and preheat for 5 minutes.
2. Meanwhile, take a 6-inches baking pan, grease it with oil and set aside.
3. Place spinach in a bowl, add remaining ingredients except for parmesan cheese, stir until well mixed and then add the mixture into prepared baking pan.
4. Open the fryer, add pan in it, close with its lid and cook for 10 minutes until cooked and cheese has melted, stirring halfway through.
5. Then sprinkle parmesan cheese on top of spinach and continue air fryer for 5 minutes at 400 degrees F until top is nicely golden and cheese has melted.
6. Serve straight away.

Nutrition Value:

- Calories: 273 Cal
- Carbs: 8 g
- Fat: 23 g
- Protein: 8 g
- Fiber: 2 g

Eggplant Parmesan

Preparation time: 20 minutes
Cooking time: 15 minutes
Servings: 4

Ingredients:

- 1/2 cup and 3 tablespoons almond flour, divided
- 1.25-pound eggplant, ½-inch sliced
- 1 tablespoon chopped parsley
- 1 teaspoon Italian seasoning
- 2 teaspoons salt
- 1 cup marinara sauce
- 1 egg, pastured
- 1 tablespoon water
- 3 tablespoons grated parmesan cheese, reduced-fat
- 1/4 cup grated mozzarella cheese, reduced-fat

Method:

1. Slice the eggplant into ½-inch pieces, place them in a colander, sprinkle with 1 ½ teaspoon salt on both sides and let it rest for 15 minutes.
2. Meanwhile, place ½ cup flour in a bowl, add egg and water and whisk until blended.
3. Place remaining flour in a shallow dish, add remaining salt, Italian seasoning, and parmesan cheese and stir until mixed.
4. Switch on the air fryer, insert fryer basket, grease it with olive oil, then shut with its lid, set the fryer at 360 degrees F and preheat for 5 minutes.
5. Meanwhile, drain the eggplant pieces, pat them dry, and then dip each slice into the egg mixture and coat with flour mixture.
6. Open the fryer, add coated eggplant slices in it in a single layer, close with its lid and cook for 8 minutes until nicely golden and cooked, flipping the eggplant slices halfway through the frying.

7. Then top each eggplant slice with a tablespoon of marinara sauce and some of the mozzarella cheese and continue air frying for 1 to 2 minutes or until cheese has melted.
8. When air fryer beeps, open its lid, transfer eggplants onto a serving plate and keep them warm.
9. Cook remaining eggplant slices in the same manner and serve.

Nutrition Value:

- Calories: 193 Cal
- Carbs: 27 g
- Fat: 5.5 g
- Protein: 10 g
- Fiber: 6 g

Cauliflower Rice

Preparation time: 10 minutes
Cooking time: 27 minutes
Servings: 3

Ingredients:

For the Tofu:

- 1 cup diced carrot
- 6 ounces tofu, extra-firm, drained
- 1/2 cup diced white onion
- 2 tablespoons soy sauce
- 1 teaspoon turmeric

For the Cauliflower:

- 1/2 cup chopped broccoli
- 3 cups cauliflower rice
- 1 tablespoon minced garlic
- 1/2 cup frozen peas
- 1 tablespoon minced ginger
- 2 tablespoons soy sauce
- 1 tablespoon apple cider vinegar
- 1 1/2 teaspoons toasted sesame oil

Method:

1. Switch on the air fryer, insert fryer pan, grease it with olive oil, then shut with its lid, set the fryer at 370 degrees F and preheat for 5 minutes.
2. Meanwhile, place tofu in a bowl, crumble it, then add remaining ingredients and stir until mixed.
3. Open the fryer, add tofu mixture in it, spray with oil, close with its lid and cook for 10 minutes until nicely golden and crispy, stirring halfway through the frying.
4. Meanwhile, place all the ingredients for cauliflower in a bowl and toss until mixed.

5. When air fryer beeps, open its lid, add cauliflower mixture, shake the pan gently to mix and continue cooking for 12 minutes, shaking halfway through the frying.
6. Serve straight away.

Nutrition Value:

- Calories: 258.1 Cal
- Carbs: 20.8 g
- Fat: 13 g
- Protein: 18.2 g
- Fiber: 7 g

Brussels Sprouts

Preparation time: 5 minutes
Cooking time: 10 minutes
Servings: 2

Ingredients:

- 2 cups Brussels sprouts
- 1/4 teaspoon sea salt
- 1 tablespoon olive oil
- 1 tablespoon apple cider vinegar

Method:

1. Switch on the air fryer, insert fryer basket, grease it with olive oil, then shut with its lid, set the fryer at 400 degrees F and preheat for 5 minutes.
2. Meanwhile, cut the sprouts lengthwise into ¼-inch thick pieces, add them in a bowl, add remaining ingredients and toss until well coated.
3. Open the fryer, add sprouts in it, close with its lid and cook for 10 minutes until crispy and cooked, shaking halfway through the frying.
4. When air fryer beeps, open its lid, transfer sprouts onto a serving plate and serve.

Nutrition Value:

- Calories: 88 Cal
- Carbs: 11 g
- Fat: 4.4 g
- Protein: 3.9 g
- Fiber: 4 g

Green Beans

Preparation time: 5 minutes
Cooking time: 13 minutes
Servings: 4

Ingredients:

- 1-pound green beans
- ¾ teaspoon garlic powder
- ¾ teaspoon ground black pepper
- 1 ¼ teaspoon salt
- ½ teaspoon paprika

Method:

1. Switch on the air fryer, insert fryer basket, grease it with olive oil, then shut with its lid, set the fryer at 400 degrees F and preheat for 5 minutes.
2. Meanwhile, place beans in a bowl, spray generously with olive oil, sprinkle with garlic powder, black pepper, salt, and paprika and toss until well coated.
3. Open the fryer, add green beans in it, close with its lid and cook for 8 minutes until nicely golden and crispy, shaking halfway through the frying.
4. When air fryer beeps, open its lid, transfer green beans onto a serving plate and serve.

Nutrition Value:

- Calories: 45 Cal
- Carbs: 7 g
- Fat: 1 g
- Protein: 2 g
- Fiber: 3 g

Asparagus Avocado Soup

Preparation time: 10 minutes
Cooking time: 20 minutes
Servings: 4

Ingredients:

- 1 avocado, peeled, pitted, cubed
- 12 ounces asparagus
- ½ teaspoon ground black pepper
- 1 teaspoon garlic powder
- 1 teaspoon sea salt
- 2 tablespoons olive oil, divided
- 1/2 of a lemon, juiced
- 2 cups vegetable stock

Method:

1. Switch on the air fryer, insert fryer basket, grease it with olive oil, then shut with its lid, set the fryer at 425 degrees F and preheat for 5 minutes.
2. Meanwhile, place asparagus in a shallow dish, drizzle with 1 tablespoon oil, sprinkle with garlic powder, salt, and black pepper and toss until well mixed.
3. Open the fryer, add asparagus in it, close with its lid and cook for 10 minutes until nicely golden and roasted, shaking halfway through the frying.
4. When air fryer beeps, open its lid and transfer asparagus to a food processor.
5. Add remaining ingredients into a food processor and pulse until well combined and smooth.
6. Tip the soup in a saucepan, pour in water if the soup is too thick and heat it over medium-low heat for 5 minutes until thoroughly heated.
7. Ladle soup into bowls and serve.

Nutrition Value:

- Calories: 208 Cal
- Carbs: 13 g
- Fat: 16 g
- Protein: 6 g
- Fiber: 5 g

Chapter 10: Fish and Seafood

Crab Cake

Preparation time: 5 minutes
Cooking time: 15 minutes
Servings: 2

Ingredients:

- 8 ounces crab meat, wild-caught
- 2 tablespoons almond flour
- 1/4 cup red bell pepper, cored, chopped
- 2 green onion, chopped
- 1 teaspoon old bay seasoning
- 1 tablespoon Dijon mustard
- 2 tablespoons mayonnaise, reduced-fat

Method:

1. Switch on the air fryer, insert fryer basket, grease it with olive oil, then shut with its lid, set the fryer at 370 degrees F and preheat for 5 minutes.
2. Meanwhile, place all the ingredients in a bowl, stir until well combined and then shape the mixture into four patties.
3. Open the fryer, add crab patties in it, spray oil over the patties, close with its lid and cook for 10 minutes until nicely golden and crispy, flipping the patties halfway through the frying.
4. When air fryer beeps, open its lid, transfer the crab patties onto a serving plate and serve with lemon wedges.

Nutrition Value:

- Calories: 123 Cal
- Carbs: 5 g
- Fat: 6 g
- Protein: 12 g
- Fiber: 1 g

Salmon

Preparation time: 5 minutes
Cooking time: 12 minutes
Servings: 2

Ingredients:

- 2 salmon fillets, wild-caught, each about 1 ½ inch thick
- 1 teaspoon ground black pepper
- 2 teaspoons paprika
- 1 teaspoon salt
- 2 teaspoons olive oil

Method:

1. Switch on the air fryer, insert fryer basket, grease it with olive oil, then shut with its lid, set the fryer at 390 degrees F and preheat for 5 minutes.
2. Meanwhile, rub each salmon fillet with oil and then season with black pepper, paprika, and salt.
3. Open the fryer, add seasoned salmon in it, close with its lid and cook for 7 minutes until nicely golden and cooked, flipping the fillets halfway through the frying.
4. When air fryer beeps, open its lid, transfer salmon onto a serving plate and serve.

Nutrition Value:

- Calories: 288 Cal
- Carbs: 1.4 g
- Fat: 18.9 g
- Protein: 28.3 g
- Fiber: 0.8 g

Parmesan Shrimp

Preparation time: 10 minutes
Cooking time: 10 minutes
Servings: 6

Ingredients:

- 2 pounds jumbo shrimp, wild-caught, peeled, deveined
- 2 tablespoons minced garlic
- 1 teaspoon onion powder
- 1 teaspoon basil
- 1 teaspoon ground black pepper
- 1/2 teaspoon dried oregano
- 2 tablespoons olive oil
- 2/3 cup grated parmesan cheese, reduced-fat
- 2 tablespoons lemon juice

Method:

1. Switch on the air fryer, insert fryer basket, grease it with olive oil, then shut with its lid, set the fryer at 350 degrees F and preheat for 5 minutes.
2. Meanwhile, place cheese in a bowl, add remaining ingredients except for shrimps and lemon juice and stir until combined.
3. Add shrimps and then toss until well coated.
4. Open the fryer, add shrimps in it, spray oil over them, close with its lid and cook for 10 minutes until nicely golden and crispy, shaking halfway through the frying.
5. When air fryer beeps, open its lid, transfer chicken onto a serving plate, drizzle with lemon juice and serve.

Nutrition Value:

- Calories: 307 Cal
- Carbs: 12 g
- Fat: 16.4 g
- Protein: 27.6 g
- Fiber: 3 g

Fish Sticks

Preparation time: 5 minutes
Cooking time: 15 minutes
Servings: 4

Ingredients:

- 1-pound cod, wild-caught
- ½ teaspoon ground black pepper
- 3/4 teaspoon Cajun seasoning
- 1 teaspoon salt
- 1 1/2 cups pork rind
- 1/4 cup mayonnaise, reduced-fat
- 2 tablespoons water
- 2 tablespoons Dijon mustard

Method:

1. Switch on the air fryer, insert fryer basket, grease it with olive oil, then shut with its lid, set the fryer at 400 degrees F and preheat for 5 minutes.
2. Meanwhile, place mayonnaise in a bowl and then whisk in water and mustard until blended.
3. Place pork rinds in a shallow dish, add Cajun seasoning, black pepper and salt and stir until mixed.
4. Cut the cod into 1 by 2 inches pieces, then dip into mayonnaise mixture and then coat with pork rind mixture.
5. Open the fryer, add fish sticks in it, spray with oil, close with its lid and cook for 10 minutes until nicely golden and crispy, flipping the sticks halfway through the frying.
6. When air fryer beeps, open its lid, transfer fish sticks onto a serving plate and serve.

Nutrition Value:

- Calories: 263 Cal
- Carbs: 1 g
- Fat: 16 g
- Protein: 26.4 g
- Fiber: 0.5 g

Shrimp with Lemon and Chile

Preparation time: 5 minutes
Cooking time: 12 minutes
Servings: 2

Ingredients:

- 1-pound shrimp, wild-caught, peeled, deveined
- 1 lemon, sliced
- 1 small red chili pepper, sliced
- ½ teaspoon ground black pepper
- 1/2 teaspoon garlic powder
- 1 teaspoon salt
- 1 tablespoon olive oil

Method:

1. Switch on the air fryer, insert fryer basket, grease it with olive oil, then shut with its lid, set the fryer at 400 degrees F and preheat for 5 minutes.
2. Meanwhile, place shrimps in a bowl, add garlic, salt, black pepper, oil, and lemon slices and toss until combined.
3. Open the fryer, add shrimps and lemon in it, close with its lid and cook for 5 minutes, shaking halfway through the frying.
4. Then add chili slices, shake the basket until mixed and continue cooking for 2 minutes or until shrimps are opaque and crispy.
5. When air fryer beeps, open its lid, transfer shrimps and lemon slices onto a serving plate and serve.

Nutrition Value:

- Calories: 112.5 Cal
- Carbs: 1 g
- Fat: 1 g
- Protein: 20.4 g
- Fiber: 0.2 g

Tilapia

Preparation time: 5 minutes
Cooking time: 12 minutes
Servings: 2

Ingredients:

- 2 tilapia fillets, wild-caught, 1 ½ inch thick
- 1 teaspoon old bay seasoning
- ¾ teaspoon lemon pepper seasoning
- ½ teaspoon salt

Method:

1. Switch on the air fryer, insert fryer basket, grease it with olive oil, then shut with its lid, set the fryer at 400 degrees F and preheat for 5 minutes.
2. Meanwhile, spray tilapia fillets with oil and then season with salt, lemon pepper, and old bay seasoning until evenly coated.
3. Open the fryer, add tilapia in it, close with its lid and cook for 7 minutes until nicely golden and cooked, turning the fillets halfway through the frying.
4. When air fryer beeps, open its lid, transfer tilapia fillets onto a serving plate and serve.

Nutrition Value:

- Calories: 36 Cal
- Carbs: 0 g
- Fat: 0.75 g
- Protein: 7.4 g
- Fiber: 0 g

Tomato Basil Scallops

Preparation time: 5 minutes
Cooking time: 15 minutes
Servings: 2

Ingredients:

- 8 jumbo sea scallops, wild-caught
- 1 tablespoon tomato paste
- 12 ounces frozen spinach, thawed and drained
- 1 tablespoon chopped fresh basil
- 1 teaspoon ground black pepper
- 1 teaspoon minced garlic
- 1 teaspoon salt
- 3/4 cup heavy whipping cream, reduced-fat

Method:

1. Switch on the air fryer, insert fryer basket, grease it with olive oil, then shut with its lid, set the fryer at 350 degrees F and preheat for 5 minutes.
2. Meanwhile, take a 7 inches baking pan, grease it with oil and place spinach in it in an even layer.
3. Spray the scallops with oil, sprinkle with ½ teaspoon each of salt and black pepper and then place scallops over the spinach.
4. Place tomato paste in a bowl, whisk in cream, basil, garlic, and remaining salt and black pepper until smooth, and then pour over the scallops.
5. Open the fryer, place the pan in it, close with its lid and cook for 10 minutes until thoroughly cooked and sauce is hot.
6. Serve straight away.

Nutrition Value:

- Calories: 359 Cal
- Carbs: 6 g
- Fat: 33 g
- Protein: 9 g
- Fiber: 1 g

Shrimp Scampi

Preparation time: 5 minutes
Cooking time: 12 minutes
Servings: 4

Ingredients:

- 1-pound shrimp, peeled, deveined
- 1 tablespoon minced garlic
- 1 tablespoon minced basil
- 1 tablespoon lemon juice
- 1 teaspoon dried chives
- 1 teaspoon dried basil
- 2 teaspoons red pepper flakes
- 4 tablespoons butter, unsalted
- 2 tablespoons chicken stock

Method:

1. Switch on the air fryer, insert fryer pan, grease it with olive oil, then shut with its lid, set the fryer at 330 degrees F and preheat for 5 minutes.
2. Add butter in it along with red pepper and garlic and cook for 2 minutes or until the butter has melted.
3. Then add remaining ingredients in the pan, stir until mixed and continue cooking for 5 minutes until shrimps have cooked, stirring halfway through.
4. When done, remove the pan from the air fryer, stir the shrimp scampi, let it rest for 1 minute and then stir again.
5. Garnish shrimps with basil leaves and serve.

Nutrition Value:

- Calories: 221 Cal
- Carbs: 1 g
- Fat: 13 g
- Protein: 23 g
- Fiber: 0 g

Salmon Cakes

Preparation time: 5 minutes
Cooking time: 12 minutes
Servings: 2

Ingredients:

- ½ cup almond flour
- 15 ounces cooked pink salmon
- ¼ teaspoon ground black pepper
- 2 teaspoons Dijon mustard
- 2 tablespoons chopped fresh dill
- 2 tablespoons mayonnaise, reduced-fat
- 1 egg, pastured
- 2 wedges of lemon

Method:

1. Switch on the air fryer, insert fryer basket, grease it with olive oil, then shut with its lid, set the fryer at 400 degrees F and preheat for 5 minutes.
2. Meanwhile, place all the ingredients in a bowl, except for lemon wedges, stir until combined and then shape into four patties, each about 4-inches.
3. Open the fryer, add salmon patties in it, spray oil over them, close with its lid and cook for 12 minutes until nicely golden and crispy, flipping the patties halfway through the frying.
4. When air fryer beeps, open its lid, transfer salmon patties onto a serving plate and serve.

Nutrition Value:

- Calories: 517 Cal
- Carbs: 15 g
- Fat: 27 g
- Protein: 52 g
- Fiber: 5 g

Cilantro Lime Shrimps

Preparation time: 25 minutes
Cooking time: 21 minutes
Servings: 4

Ingredients:

- 1/2-pound shrimp, peeled, deveined
- 1/2 teaspoon minced garlic
- 1 tablespoon chopped cilantro
- 1/2 teaspoon paprika
- ¾ teaspoon salt
- 1/2 teaspoon ground cumin
- 2 tablespoons lemon juice

Method:

1. Take 6 wooden skewers and let them soak in warm water for 20 minutes.
2. Meanwhile, switch on the air fryer, insert fryer basket, grease it with olive oil, then shut with its lid, set the fryer at 350 degrees F and let preheat.
3. Whisk together lemon juice, paprika, salt, cumin, and garlic in a large bowl, then add shrimps and toss until well coated.
4. Drain the skewers and then thread shrimps in them.
5. Open the fryer, add shrimps in it in a single layer, spray oil over them, close with its lid and cook for 8 minutes until nicely golden and cooked, turning the skewers halfway through the frying.
6. When air fryer beeps, open its lid, transfer shrimps onto a serving plate and keep them warm.
7. Cook remaining shrimp skewers in the same manner and serve.

Nutrition Value:

- Calories: 59 Cal
- Carbs: 0.3 g
- Fat: 1.5 g
- Protein: 11 g
- Fiber: 0 g

Chapter 11: Dessert

Cheesecake Bites

Preparation time: 40 minutes
Cooking time: 9 minutes
Servings: 4

Ingredients:

- 1/2 cup almond flour
- 1/2 cup and 2 tablespoons erythritol sweetener, divided
- 8 ounces cream cheese, reduced-fat, softened
- 1/2 teaspoon vanilla extract, unsweetened
- 4 tablespoons heavy cream, reduced-fat, divided

Method:

1. Prepare the cheesecake mixture and for this, place softened cream cheese in a bowl, add cream, vanilla, and ½ cup sweetener and whisk using an electric mixer until smooth.
2. Scoop the mixture on a baking sheet lined with parchment sheet, then place it in the freezer for 30 minutes until firm.
3. Place flour in a small bowl and stir in remaining sweetener.
4. Then switch on the air fryer, insert fryer basket, grease it with olive oil, then shut with its lid, set the fryer at 350 degrees F and preheat for 5 minutes.
5. Meanwhile, cut the cheesecake mix into bite-size pieces and then coat with almond flour mixture.
6. Open the fryer, add cheesecake bites in it, close with its lid and cook for 2 minutes until nicely golden and crispy.
7. Serve straight away.

Nutrition Value:

- Calories: 198 Cal
- Carbs: 6 g
- Fat: 18 g
- Protein: 3 g
- Fiber: 0 g

Coconut Pie

Preparation time: 5 minutes
Cooking time: 45 minutes
Servings: 6

Ingredients:

- 1/2 cup coconut flour
- 1/2 cup erythritol sweetener
- 1 cup shredded coconut, unsweetened, divided
- 1/4 cup butter, unsalted
- 1 1/2 teaspoon vanilla extract, unsweetened
- 2 eggs, pastured
- 1 1/2 cups milk, low-fat, unsweetened
- ¼ cup shredded coconut, toasted

Method:

1. Switch on the air fryer, insert fryer basket, grease it with olive oil, then shut with its lid, set the fryer at 350 degrees F and preheat for 5 minutes.
2. Meanwhile, place all the ingredients in a bowl and whisk until well blended and smooth batter comes together.
3. Take a 6-inches pie pan, grease it oil, then pour in the prepared batter and smooth the top.
4. Open the fryer, place the pie pan in it, close with its lid and cook for 45 minutes until pie has set and inserted a toothpick into the pie slide out clean.
5. When air fryer beeps, open its lid, take out the pie pan and let it cool.
6. Garnish the pie with toasted coconut, then cut into slices and serve.

Nutrition Value:

- Calories: 236 Cal
- Carbs: 16 g
- Fat: 16 g
- Protein: 3 g
- Fiber: 2 g

Crustless Cheesecake

Preparation time: 5 minutes
Cooking time: 10 minutes
Servings: 2

Ingredients:

- 16 ounces cream cheese, reduced-fat, softened
- 2 tablespoons sour cream, reduced-fat
- 3/4 cup erythritol sweetener
- 1 teaspoon vanilla extract, unsweetened
- 2 eggs, pastured
- 1/2 teaspoon lemon juice

Method:

1. Switch on the air fryer, insert fryer basket, grease it with olive oil, then shut with its lid, set the fryer at 350 degrees F and preheat for 5 minutes.
2. Meanwhile, take two 4 inches springform pans, grease them with oil and set aside.
3. Crack the eggs in a bowl and then whisk in lemon juice, sweetener and vanilla until smooth.
4. Whisk in cream cheese and sour cream until blended and then divide the mixture evenly between prepared pans.
5. Open the fryer, place pans in it, close with its lid and cook for 10 minutes until cakes are set and inserted skewer into the cakes slide out clean.
6. When air fryer beeps, open its lid, take out the cake pans and let cakes cool in them.
7. Take out the cakes, refrigerate for 3 hours until cooled and then serve.

Nutrition Value:

- Calories: 318 Cal
- Carbs: 1 g
- Fat: 29.7 g
- Protein: 11.7 g
- Fiber: 0 g

Chocolate Cake

Preparation time: 5 minutes
Cooking time: 15 minutes
Servings: 6

Ingredients:

- 1/4 cup coconut flour
- 1 teaspoon baking powder
- 1/3 cup truvia sweetener
- 1/4 teaspoon salt
- 2 tablespoon cocoa powder, unsweetened
- 1 teaspoon vanilla extract, unsweetened
- 4 tablespoons butter, unsalted, melted
- 3 eggs, pastured
- 1/2 cup heavy whipping cream, reduced-fat

Method:

1. Switch on the air fryer, insert fryer basket, grease it with olive oil, then shut with its lid, set the fryer at 350 degrees F and preheat for 5 minutes.
2. Meanwhile, take a 6 cups muffin pan, grease it with oil and set aside until required.
3. Place melted butter in a bowl, whisk in sweetener until blended and then beat in vanilla, eggs, and cream until combined.
4. Add remaining ingredients, beat again until incorporated and smooth batter comes together and then pour the mixture into prepared pan.
5. Open the fryer, place the pan in it, close with its lid and cook for 10 minutes until cake is done and inserted skewer into the cake slides out clean.
6. When air fryer beeps, open its lid, take out the cake pan and let the cake cool in it.
7. Take out the cakes, cut it into pieces, and serve.

Nutrition Value:

- Calories: 192 Cal
- Carbs: 8 g
- Fat: 16 g
- Protein: 4 g
- Fiber: 2 g

Chocolate Brownies

Preparation time: 10 minutes
Cooking time: 45 minutes
Servings: 4

Ingredients:

- 1/2 cup chocolate chips, sugar-free
- 1 teaspoon vanilla extract, unsweetened
- 1/4 cup erythritol sweetener
- 1/2 cup butter, unsalted
- 3 eggs, pastured

Method:

1. Switch on the air fryer, insert fryer basket, grease it with olive oil, then shut with its lid, set the fryer at 350 degrees F and preheat for 10 minutes.
2. Meanwhile, place chocolate and butter in a heatproof bowl and microwave for 1 minute or until chocolate has melted, stirring every 30 seconds.
3. Crack eggs in another bowl, beat in vanilla and sweetener until smooth and then slowly beat in melted chocolate mixture until well incorporated.
4. Take a springform pan that fits into the air fryer, grease it with oil and then pour in batter in it.
5. Open the fryer, place the pan in it, close with its lid and cook for 35 minutes until cake is done and inserted toothpick into the brownies slide out clean.
6. When air fryer beeps, open its lid, take out the pan and let the brownies cool in it.
7. Then take out the brownies, cut it into even pieces, and serve.

Nutrition Value:

- Calories: 224 Cal
- Carbs: 3 g
- Fat: 23 g
- Protein: 4 g
- Fiber: 1 g

Spiced Apples

Preparation time: 5 minutes
Cooking time: 17 minutes
Servings: 4

Ingredients:

- 4 small apples, cored, sliced
- 2 tablespoons erythritol sweetener
- 1 teaspoon apple pie spice
- 2 tablespoons olive oil

Method:

1. Switch on the air fryer, insert fryer basket, grease it with olive oil, then shut with its lid, set the fryer at 350 degrees F and preheat for 5 minutes.
2. Meanwhile, place apple slice in a bowl, sprinkle with sweetener and spice, and drizzle with oil and stir until evenly coated.
3. Open the fryer, add apple slices in it, close with its lid and cook for 12 minutes until nicely golden and crispy, shaking halfway through the frying.
4. Serve straight away.

Nutrition Value:

- Calories: 89.6 Cal
- Carbs: 21.8 g
- Fat: 2 g
- Protein: 0.5 g
- Fiber: 5.3 g

Sweet Potato Fries

Preparation time: 5 minutes
Cooking time: 13 minutes
Servings: 4

Ingredients:

- 2 medium sweet potatoes, peeled
- 1 tablespoon arrowroot starch
- 2 tablespoons cinnamon
- 1/4 cup coconut sugar
- 2 teaspoons melted butter, unsalted
- ½ tablespoon olive oil
- Confectioner's swerve as needed

Method:

1. Switch on the air fryer, insert fryer basket, grease it with olive oil, then shut with its lid, set the fryer at 370 degrees F and preheat for 5 minutes.
2. Meanwhile, cut peeled sweet potatoes into ½-inch thick slices, then place them in a bowl, add oil and starch and toss until well coated.
3. Open the fryer, add sweet potatoes in it, close with its lid and cook for 8 minutes until nicely golden, shaking halfway through the frying.
4. When air fryer beeps, open its lid, transfer sweet potato fries in a bowl, add butter, sprinkle with sugar and cinnamon and toss until well mixed.
5. Sprinkle confectioner's swerve on the fries and serve.

Nutrition Value:

- Calories: 130 Cal
- Carbs: 27 g
- Fat: 2.3 g
- Protein: 1.2 g
- Fiber: 3 g

Chocolate Lava Cake

Preparation time: 5 minutes
Cooking time: 13 minutes
Servings: 2

Ingredients:

- 1 tablespoon flax meal
- 1/2 teaspoon baking powder
- 2 tablespoons cocoa powder, unsweetened
- 2 tablespoons erythritol sweetener
- 1/8 teaspoon Stevia sweetener
- 1/8 teaspoon vanilla extract, unsweetened
- 1 tablespoon olive oil
- 2 tablespoons water
- 1 egg, pastured

Method:

1. Switch on the air fryer, insert fryer basket, grease it with olive oil, then shut with its lid, set the fryer at 350 degrees F and preheat for 5 minutes.
2. Meanwhile, take a two cups ramekin, grease it with oil and set aside.
3. Place all the ingredients in a bowl, whisk until well combined and incorporated and pour the batter into the ramekin.
4. Open the fryer, place ramekin in it, close with its lid and cook for 8 minutes until cake is done and inserted skewer into the cake slides out clean.
5. When air fryer beeps, open its lid, take out the ramekin and let the cake cool in it.
6. Then take out the cake, cut it into slices, and serve.

Nutrition Value:

- Calories: 362.8 Cal
- Carbs: 3.4 g
- Fat: 33.6 g
- Protein: 11.7 g
- Fiber: 0.6 g

Conclusion

The air fryer is a savior for those who want to have their meals ready in about 15 minutes. It's a great option for seniors who don't want to strain their hands for doing meal prepping and cooking on hot stove. For college students, air fryer is an ultimate snack-maker, especially when they are busy in assignments or when it is late night, and food mess is closed. Moreover, easy cooking with the air fryer motivates single to cook fresh foods and that too in small amount in just minutes at their homes. It motivates eating healthier and saving money that is wasted in eating out. And, it is definitely for those people who don't like to cook. With the air fryer, you can toss frozen ingredients in it like chicken wings, steaks, pre-cut vegetables or even pizza and cook them in minutes.

Most importantly, air fryer is a breath of relief for people with diabetes who are struggling with their diet routine and trying to control their craving for fried foods.

Made in the USA
Columbia, SC
08 February 2020